IN THE THICK OF IT

MASTERING THE ART OF LEADING FROM THE
MIDDLE

GWYN TEATRO

Jane,
Hope you enjoy!
Gwyn

Copyright @2019 Gwyn Teatro

Published by Ingenium Books Publishing Inc.

Toronto, Ontario, Canada M6P 1Z2

All rights reserved.

ingeniumbooks.com

Ingenium Books supports copyright. Copyright fuels innovation and creativity, encourages diverse voices, promotes free speech, and helps create vibrant culture. Thank you for purchasing an authorized edition of this book and for complying with copyright laws by not reproducing, scanning, or distributing this book or any part of it without permission. You are supporting writers and helping ensure Ingenium Books can continue to publish nonfiction books for readers like you. You are permitted to excerpt brief quotations in a review.

ISBNs

Paperback: 978-1-989059-25-8

eBook: 978-1-989059-26-5

Hardcover: 978-1-989059-27-2

Audiobook: 978-1-989059-28-9

Edited by: Boni Wagner-Stafford, Ingenium books

Author photo credit: Tamea Byrd Photography

PRAISE FOR IN THE THICK OF IT

After years of working in the corporate world, I'm all-too-familiar with top-down leadership. In my own workshops on "How to Manage Your Boss," I teach employees how to *manage up* in their organizations. But until I read this book, I'd never heard of *leading from the middle*. What a great concept! Read it and reap ... great results!

—*BJ GALLAGHER*, COAUTHOR, *"A PEACOCK IN THE LAND OF PENGUINS: A FABLE ABOUT CREATIVITY AND COURAGE"*

Reading **In the Thick of It** is like sipping a cup of coffee with a trusted friend who knows you well and knows what you need. Gwyn Teatro's immensely readable book covers a lot of terrain, but is so easy and fun to read, you don't want to put it down. Through a combination of excellent, practical advice and thought-provoking questions, you will be guided toward becoming the leader and person you were meant to be.

—*JESSE LYN STONER*, FOUNDER OF SEAPORT CENTRE FOR COLLABORATIVE LEADERSHIP. CO-AUTHOR OF THE BEST-SELLING BOOK "FULL STEAM AHEAD!"

This is more than a book about leadership – it's about making a choice to lead, to tackle change head-on, and to drive change when necessary. The toolkit Gwyn delivers is powerful, yet practical. The stories and examples clearly illustrate what it takes to lead effectively. **In The Thick of It** is a must-read for anyone looking to grow as a leader.

—*LISA KING*, AUTHOR, JUST DO YOU: AUTHENTICITY, LEADERSHIP, AND YOUR PERSONAL BRAND. PRESIDENT, DANELI PARTNERS

In the Thick of It takes the new or experienced leader on a practical and realistic journey of learning and reinforcement. Leadership can be improved and developed by most of us, however it is often the 'how' that limits potential. Gwyn has brilliantly compiled a book that will assist in understanding how you can be a more effective leader. **In the Thick of It** will add value to anyone who wishes to influence others, in or out of the workplace. Congratulations to Gwyn and you, the reader!

—*STEVE RIDDLE*, DIRECTOR/COACH/MENTOR/LEADER,
COACHSTATION, BRISBANE, AUSTRALIA

I had a tough time trying to capture what I love about this book in two sentences. Congratulations -- you have created something really special! This book is so well written, has so many gems of wisdom, teaches without preaching, shares great stories we will remember, and covers so many topics near and dear to my heart, like developing self-awareness, leading through change, and building strength through struggle. So why is this a problem for me? Because I can't do this book justice in a sentence or two, other than to say—read this book and share it! Best book on learning how to be a leader I've read in ages. And the Think About It questions quite literally make us think about who we are, what we know, and what we are learning from this amazing book that will make a difference in our leadership ability, and in our lives.

—*KAT TANSEY*, CHANGE AGENT, EDUCATOR AT
WWW.RESILIENTHERO.COM. AUTHOR OF CHOOSING TO BE

Told from the heart, Gwyn Teatro's narratives are crammed full of insights that will inspire you. Firmly grounded in the reality of the joys and the adversity we all face in our lives, she shows how exercising uplifting leadership will give us meaning in our families, our communities, our workplace, and ultimately in ourselves.

—*HUBERT SAINT-ONGE*, SAINTONGE ALLIANCE

I am a long-time fan of Gwyn Teatro's posts on leadership and expected her book to be the essential Kitchen Table Wisdom for managers and leaders. Gwyn delivered. Picture yourself reading this book in your most comfortable chair, fireplace glowing, beverage of choice by your side. It is rich in practical wisdom about the very real situations managers and leaders face, presented with sincerity, warmth and humor. **In the Thick of It** begins with a poem that reveals Gwyn's vision of what is possible and worth leading for. It is pure inspiration and pure Gwyn - the Dr. Seuss of leadership.

—DR ANNE PERSCHEL, *FOUNDER & PRESIDENT, GERMANE COACHING AND CONSULTING*

In The Thick Of It offers managers who feel stuck in the middle, a road map to not just succeed, but thrive as leaders.

—TANVEER NASEER, *MSC., AUTHOR, "LEADERSHIP VERTIGO" AND INC. 100 LEADERSHIP SPEAKER*

Most business books are written for the CEO at the tippy-top of the org chart. CEOs can choose the people on their team, change strategy, and pretty much do as they please. The rest of us are in the middle. We work with the team we've got, implement the strategy someone else concocted, and answer to people in all directions. Gwyn Teatro has written a book for the rest of us. You'll learn how to lead from the middle. You'll also learn how to get from where you are now to where you'd like to be.

—WALLY BOCK, *AUTHOR, "NOW YOU'RE THE BOSS: MAKING THE MOST OF THE MOST IMPORTANT TRANSITION IN BUSINESS." BLOGGER AT THREE START LEADERSHIP.*

I've loved reading Gwyn Teatro's take on the workplace and managing and leading for years, and was ecstatic to know she had written a book. ***In the Thick of It: Mastering the Art of Leading from the Middle*** blends Gwyn's fabulous, engaging writing with cogent guidance and examples on what it means to lead effectively from the toughest spot of all—the middle. A joy to read and an excellent guide for everyone involved in supporting the work of others.

*—**ART PETTY**, FOUNDER ART PETTY GROUP*

Simple. Clear. Relatable. Actionable. Gwyn provides an insightful guide for the many who are called to lead by choice or by circumstance from the most challenging vantage point of all – the middle!

*—**SUSAN MAZZA**, CEO CLARUS CONSULTING GROUP LLC, LEADERSHIP COACH, FACILITATOR OF ORGANIZATIONAL CHANGE.*

Gwyn Teatro has a wealth of experience in the leadership and HR sphere. She is able to tap into a well of richness, to share anecdotes that highlight all the nuances and contradictions of the modern workplace. Her practical tips will help aspiring, and established leaders, navigate the ambiguities they face on a daily basis.

Today's organizations are fast paced, complex and ever changing. Gwyn's style is relaxed and accessible. She reminds us, with a smile, that leadership comes in many forms, but respect, purpose, trust, relationships, recognition, growth and shared values are essential components to forming an inclusive team. A great resource for anyone at any point in their career!

*—**DOROTHY DALTON**, INTERNATIONAL TALENT MANAGEMENT STRATEGIST AND CEO, 3PLUS INTERNATIONAL LTD.*

To Don, with whom I have had many a "Teatro adventure." Thank you for this one. It would not have been possible without you.

CONTENTS

If I Ran the Zoo		xi
Leading from the Middle		xiii
SECTION I: CHOOSING TO LEAD		xvii
1.	Choosing to Lead	1
2.	Changing the Narrative	17
3.	Leading on Purpose	27
	SECTION II: COMMUNICATION	41
4.	A Fly in the Ointment of Progress	43
5.	Transmission	55
6.	Reception	75
	SECTION III: WORKING TOGETHER	91
7.	Working together	93
8.	Collaboration	107
9.	Leading Teams	119
	SECTION IV: LEADING THROUGH CHANGE	131
10.	The Challenge of Change	133
11.	Know Thyself	147
12.	Building Support	159
13.	Fertilizing the Change Environment	173
14.	Getting to Action	185
15.	Building Strength Through Struggle	197
	Now's the Time	207
	If You Liked "In the Thick of It"	211
	Acknowledgments	213
	About the Author	217
	Reading References	219
	Notes	225

IF I RAN THE ZOO

With apologies to Dr. Seuss.

If I ran the zoo,
I'd begin with the view
That my organization includes you, and you.
All manner of folk, both women and men
All shapes and sizes, all cultures and then...
I'd paint a big picture up there on the wall
A picture so clear it would dazzle, enthrall
All those wonderful folk with their heads full of notions
Who want to commit with their hearts and emotions.
If I ran the zoo, I would see to it, too
What's important to me is important to you.
And just to be sure, I'd turn it around
So things that you value, with me, would resound.
Then we'd roll up our sleeves and get down to work
With genuine effort...no one would shirk.
With good conversations and tough ones as well
There'd be no need to shout or to curse or to yell.
If I ran the zoo, there'd be elephants too
But not in the room 'cuz between me and you
A room with an elephant's crowded I think
(And after a while, the room starts to stink.)
And speaking of animals, there'd be *octopi*,
With tentacles reaching way up to the sky
Crossing all kinds of boundaries, and silos and such
To change for the better the world we all touch.
If I ran the zoo, I would hire people who
Would focus on making our customers, too
Feel glad that they know us and to want to come back
And we'd work to make sure there'd be nothing they'd lack
We'd be curious, too, us folks in this zoo
We'd want to be knowing the why, what and who
Of what happens around us and how it takes place
'Cuz, change is a creature we have to embrace.
So, that's what I'd do, if I ran the zoo.
There's more... but I'll turn it over to you.
With blank sheet of paper and pen in the ink,
Tell me, how would you do it?
What do you think?

LEADING FROM THE MIDDLE

We've never met but it's possible I know you. You are in the middle of everything. Some people might describe you as part of the sandwich generation, wedged between two groups of family members whose demands keep you constantly on the hop.

At work you are also in the middle. You are a boss. You *have* a boss, most probably more than one. Being in the middle, in the thick of it, can be interesting. It can also be difficult, tedious and exhausting.

I know that feeling.

Years ago, I worked for a very large bank in Toronto. I had bosses. I was a boss to a few others. Also, as manager, personnel services for the international region of the bank, I had a sizeable portfolio of internal clients to whom I consulted.

The HR department was kind of like a rabbit warren, a maze of connecting spaces partitioned off by half walls, carpeted to cut the general din of a busy workplace. My personal office was nowhere near a window and my presence in it could only be detected by the trail of cigarette smoke that rose at regular intervals, as if to give signal I was still in there somewhere.

The work was satisfying enough. I liked my immediate bosses. It paid my rent and kept me in coffee and cigarettes, which in combination had become staples in my diet. I didn't feel I had the luxury to ask myself if *satisfying enough* was indeed enough or just simply all I thought I deserved. I needed not to be troubled by such unruly thoughts. There was so much else going on in my life that I needed *this*, my job, to be stable. And yet, changes at work were afoot and while I didn't know for sure, my spidey sense told me I would not be exempt from being chosen for the somewhat alarmingly popular process of downsizing or right-sizing or whatever euphemism there is for being fired. It wasn't imminent, but it was coming. I could feel it.

At home, there was turmoil. My husband and I were in the middle of a very unpleasant divorce. Are there any pleasant ones? Our family of four was divided in half with my husband and teenaged son living in one place, and I, and our youngest son, in another several miles away.

We lived like that for a couple of years. Every other weekend, the little one went to stay with his dad. Every other weekend on his return, I was made aware of my inadequacies and reminded in some way that my place in hell was most assuredly reserved. As time went on, I began to believe it.

It was about then that the question of *satisfying enough* ceased to become a luxury and instead became a necessary inquiry into not only my work but also my life. Was I going to allow myself to feel stuck in the middle with *no* choice? Or, was I going to accept that there is *always* a choice and make one that would expand my place in the middle and also help me to break out of an unsustainable situation?

It's not an uncommon dilemma. Our stories will be different and our sandwich ingredients will vary, but sometimes I expect you wonder if *where you are* is all there is, or going to be. Yet, for you, there is hardly time for spidey senses to kick in because the changes imposed upon you are unrelenting.

This is the way of the twenty-first century, it seems. It asks you to be flexible while making demands on your day as if there were more than twenty-four hours available. It affects those you lead and those you love, whether you like it or not.

How did this happen?

Well, somewhere along the way the world got smaller and the pace of it faster. Technology took care of many of the mundane tasks. In their place, enterprises of all description chose to engage in new ventures that required more and more of your time. Transactions between countries that once took months to complete are now finished in a matter of minutes, even seconds. Simply put, instead of permitting some of the spaces technology created to lay fallow and allow for a breath or two, we chose to fill them all, cranking up the speed and demanding everyone to keep up. As a result, the little hamster has no time to fall asleep in the wheel.

Along with the exciting prospects this accelerated society affords, we have created equally new and more complex challenges.

You are a leader in the middle of it all. You want to be the kind of leader that encourages others to do, and be, their best. You imagine yourself accomplishing something great, something that has meaning, not just for you but for others too. In your ideal world, people are not cogs in a wheel that rolls dispassionately toward the bottom line. They are like you and I, searching for something that gives them purpose.

If some of this sounds familiar, take heart. Because from your place in the middle, there is opportunity. After all, the middle is a place where most of us live and learn. It is what we choose to do with it that makes the difference between feeling sandwiched and expanding our horizons, pushing out from the centre and creating larger, more productive and satisfying spaces. Nothing about it is easy, but it is entirely possible. And the feeling you get when you do it? Well, that is so much better than *satisfying enough*.

SECTION I: CHOOSING TO LEAD

1

CHOOSING TO LEAD

Let's first establish that leadership is a choice we make, regardless of whether we have been formally acknowledged as a leader. It's unwise to assume because people have been given formal leadership roles, they actually enjoy the challenges leading presents. Neither can we assume that those who have no designated leadership title have no leadership skill or opportunity.

In this chapter we're going to explore the question: what *is* leadership? It's a question with so few words and yet when asked, invites an overabundance of opinion. If you look up the word *leadership* in any dictionary, a common definition includes, "the act of leading a group or an organization." Oversimplified, but that seems about right even so.

This definition also includes reference to leaders of countries, directors, governors and kings (with minor mention of queens somewhere in the mix). Synonyms provided for the word *leader* include chief, captain, authority figure, and commander. So it's not surprising that when we consider what leadership is, our minds go first to the rarified air of the captains of industry, the wealthy philanthropists, and those occupying huge glass-walled corner offices on the top floor of large global corporations. We are certain leadership comes with daunting complexity and a whiff of command and control. From this viewpoint, in fact, the notion of leadership can seem a stretch for those of us in the middle who lead and are also led. As well, there are some who would have us believe that leadership is only for a select few.

They would be wrong.

In truth, leadership is available to all of us. It doesn't always come with a title or a private office, but it's there. And it asks us to do something with it. Of course, the more we learn about it, the more likely we are to make it a conscious choice.

However, if you think you must have a natural ability to lead others in order to be a leader, I say this: There will always be people whose personalities have drawing power, a certain charisma that's hard to deny. It doesn't make them good leaders. It only gives them the gift of a willing audience. The work of leadership begins after that.

Regardless of your personality or your designated position, you can lead. If you have the focus, the will, and the courage it requires, it is entirely possible for you to be a good leader, even a great one, with or without charisma, with or without position power.

To begin, there are two fundamental things that leadership is *not*.

1. Leadership is Not About You

Real leadership happens when your role as a leader becomes about something other than yourself. Your individual importance is overshadowed by the purpose you serve. Evidence of your leadership emerges through the quality of your relationships with colleagues and subordinates and the calibre of the work they produce.

This kind of leadership asks that you give others what they need to do their best. It invites you to guide, coach, and challenge them. It requires you to be clear about your collective goals and provide the necessary boundaries within which people can produce optimal work. It expects you to clear obstacles that lie in the way of progress toward fulfillment of your common purpose. And, in return, this kind of leadership will demand everyone's best effort and hold them accountable for the work they do.

2. Leadership is Not About Being a Hero

 No institution can possibly survive if it needs geniuses or supermen to manage it. It must be organized in such a way as to be able to get along under a leadership composed of average human beings.

PETER DRUCKER

Most of us are just that: average human beings. Sometimes all it takes is to believe in something enough to be willing to go first.

Leadership is about caring. It is about doing and participating. If you expect perfection from it, or from yourself in the pursuit of it, you will be disappointed. If you spend your time looking to the few for answers, you miss the opportunity to find your own answers and to explore possibilities that can only be found in the brainpower of the many.

So if leadership isn't about charisma, or being a hero, or indeed about you at all, what is it?

Leadership is a Science and an Art

There is a great deal of data available on the science of leadership. This research is crucial to the development and effectiveness of organizations. Often, what comes out of the research provides useful information and tools for leaders to know and employ in the effective running of an enterprise. Yet, when it gets right down to it, once the science of systems and processes are in place, it's the art of leadership that makes the difference between success and failure.

The art of leadership is imprecise. It doesn't come with a set of rules. Choosing leadership asks a lot of you. It asks you to draw lines and strive for balance between elements that have opposing impact.

For instance, it asks you to be bold without being obnoxious; to be willing to risk rejections, to bend rules and make new ones. It also asks you to explore uncharted waters and to resist the belief that only your own views count. It asks you to be resilient without being stubborn; to learn to cope with stress, disappointment, and criticism; to bounce back from adversity but to maintain a level of vulnerability that allows you to express your emotions; to show your humanity and accept the things you need to know about yourself.

It also asks you to be tolerant without being a pushover; to listen to and learn from opposing views but to challenge those that work against your common purpose or values. It further demands that you be tough without being callous; to hold yourself and others accountable for the decisions you make but do so in such a way that creates lessons rather than metes out punishment.

Sometimes, it even asks you not to lead but to follow, to see skill in someone else that you don't have and to put aside your ego for the sake of a better outcome.

When you choose leadership, learn the science by all means, but work hard on developing the art. Because this is what separates the wheat from the chaff.

Leadership is a Way of Being

There is a mercurial element in the notion of leadership as a *way of being*. It requires us to be aware of what's going on around us enough to know when leading by going first is called for or when following or collaborating with peers is going to get the job done better. There are a number of hats involved and none screwed down so tightly to our heads that it suggests strict devotion to one particular style. However, in choosing leadership as a way of being, you make yourself aware of the impact you have on others and the example you set through your behaviour. You don't have to have position power for that.

Leading by example is something we all do on a daily basis. We use that phrase, *leading by example*, a lot in organizations with the expectation that the examples we set will always be good ones. Yet, there are times when we manage to muck it up or make assumptions about what it really means.

• • •

ASSUMPTION #1: IF I'M SEEN DOING THE RIGHT THINGS, THAT WILL BE ENOUGH.

Some think leading by example is not a way of *being* but a way of *doing*. They appreciate that in order to engage people at the office, they have to serve as a role model. And so, they create a model of personal behaviour that may have little or no bearing on who they really are. In effect, they put on their office persona in the morning along with their business clothes and take it off again when they get home and change into something more comfortable. This practice is not sustainable over time. It's exhausting, and leaders who engage in this charade are eventually found out.

ASSUMPTION #2: DO AS I SAY, NOT AS I DO.

Some think you can get people to do as you say and not as you do, as long as you don't get caught.

Ask Bill about that. Bill was a board member in charge of building maintenance projects for our condominium complex. He had opinions about everything and was never shy to express them. When he spoke, people tended to listen because he looked like a stereotypical boss: tall with greying hair and a rather imperious demeanour. As well, Bill's voice had an authoritarian timbre that made you pay attention even when he was talking rubbish.

One day Bill passed down a stern edict to those of us who had installed weather-stripping to the bottom of our front doors to minimize drafts. Apparently, the weather stripping was interfering with the flow of air throughout the building. Bill was quite clear that this couldn't go on and instructed all such weather stripping to be removed post-haste.

Some time later, another board member had reason to slip a note under Bill's front door. The attempt proved unsuccessful, as the weather-stripping Bill had installed blocked both the note and the flow of air from entering his suite.

It was a small thing. But it cast a negative light on the man and undermined both his credibility and any trust he might previously have earned.

· · ·

ASSUMPTION #3: PEOPLE ONLY SEE WHAT I WANT THEM TO SEE.

There is a belief among some leaders that people will only pick up and emulate the behaviours they want others to adopt. But here's the thing. No matter who you are, as long as you are alive, someone will be looking to you for an example of how to behave in certain circumstances. Even if you have never been placed in a formal leadership role, you influence those around you simply by being there. And, being human, you are not always going to act in exemplary fashion.

Witness the time when I was invited to attend a luncheon in the head office executive dining room of the bank. This was a hallowed place where only top executives and their guests were allowed. Portraits of past important bank presidents and chairmen adorned the oak-panelled walls. They stared coldly down from their lofty places as if auditing the manners of those who sat around the table.

I knew this place existed but had never before seen it. Needless to say, the invitation came as a surprise. After all, I was a junior personnel assistant. How had this come about?

The purpose of the luncheon was to entertain a party of Chinese students. On meeting them I began to realize why I might have been chosen to participate. The students were all rather small and I, also being rather small, seemed to be the only bank representative who could look them straight in the eye without having to sit down.

The dining room looked lovely (wall-mounted imperious past presidents notwithstanding). The table was set with the finest china and crystal glassware and adorned with several simple and pretty flower arrangements.

The students were polite to the point of being deferential. They wore the uniform required of the then-Chinese communist regime and were doing their best to converse using the little English they knew. It was decidedly better than the zero Mandarin any of us knew, so it's safe to say it wasn't the most comfortable setting for them. I wasn't exactly in my element either. Nonetheless, we managed to get along quite well without either causing or being the source of embarrassment. So far so good.

Then we were invited to sit down. On doing so, my diminutive companions and I discovered that the table was quite high and the chairs, in contrast, quite low. In spite of this, we managed well enough. Until we were served dessert.

There were fresh strawberries arranged in tall-stemmed glasses rimmed with sugar. It didn't take long for me to discover that if I actually wanted to eat my dessert, I would have to stand up. My lunch companions seemed to be in the same predicament. And yet, the draw of the delicious strawberries was very great. And so, at what I considered to be a strategic moment, I took up my spoon, stood up very quickly, popped a strawberry into my mouth and sat down just as quickly to chew and swallow it.

Very shortly thereafter, my new companions followed my lead. Soon, all the small humans around that table were popping up and down until together we looked as though we were moving to the beat of an oompah band.

I was never invited to eat in the executive dining room again.

To be honest, I'm not sure I would have done things differently in this case because leadership as a way of being asks you to be *you*, not an imagined or expected version of you. Sometimes you will set an example you didn't intend. You will make mistakes. But whether you have a designated title and the attending formal responsibilities, or you are in charge of a volunteer committee in your community, it's always a good idea to be mindful of your impact on others.

Leadership is More Jazz Than Symphony

 I used to think that running an organization was equivalent to conducting a symphony orchestra. But I don't think that's quite it. It's more like jazz. There is more improvisation.

WARREN BENNIS, SCHOLAR, AUTHOR OF BOOKS ON
ORGANIZATIONAL BEHAVIOUR

I must confess. I really like the symphony orchestra metaphor, simply because it is beautifully uncluttered. Yet, as much as I would like to think it possible for all things to be in harmony at all times, I know (and you know) the reality to be a lot messier, or jazzier, metaphorically speaking. In fact it is perhaps the jazz of life, the stuff requiring spontaneity and improvisation that transforms the vanilla of a well-ordered enterprise into something spiced with possibility and potential for greatness.

So it is with leadership.

In leadership, there are times for following a well-planned strategy and times when doing so isn't going to work. The landscape has a way of changing rapidly, often requiring leaders, as creative beings, to rely on instinct to successfully navigate unexpected events and explore unknown places.

At those times, improvisation is a useful tool. However, as with jazz, improvisation on its own will not create a joyful noise. It must somehow find its way back to the primary melody no matter how far afield it may go.

In leadership, the primary melody lies in the organizational vision, its purpose, operating principles and the clarity of shared goals. How far afield we are willing to go to realize the vision and fulfill the purpose is usually dependent on how much we know.

Knowledge is power. It's almost become a catch phrase that causes us to nod our heads dutifully, often with a tinge of cynicism. Nevertheless, we might do well to unroll our eyes because there is something very substantive about knowledge as a tool of power. It goes beyond learning for its own sake and causes us to see the value in engaging our curiosity and widening our perspectives. In truth, the more curious we are and the more we seek to learn about our immediate environment and the world around us, the better equipped we are to improvise while making decisions that actually serve the collective purpose.

People accomplish this in a variety of ways. The adventurous ones climb mountains or set sail on voyages around the world. Some leave the comfort of their home country and move to places where the culture varies greatly from their own. These people return from their adventures bringing with them a whole new perspective on how the world works. It's not uncommon. New knowledge can do that to a person as we learn to appreciate things we were ignorant about before. We also learn the boundlessness of things we still don't know. It is as humbling as it is enlightening. And, it proffers the kind of education that expands the worldview in a way that no bricks-and-mortar educational institution could match.

Of course not everyone has the temperament, opportunity, or stamina to set sail to parts unknown, climb Everest, or move to a foreign country. There is a window of opportunity for this that opens briefly and tends to close quickly on those of us who hesitate.

Given this, how can we venture beyond the world behind our front doors? How do we push our boundaries and invite a richer level of knowledge to expand not only our minds but also our ability to think past the confines of our current reality?

1. READ WIDELY AND ENCOURAGE OTHERS TO DO THE SAME

Those who read a wide variety of material seem better able to make bigger picture connections. I'm not talking about just reading business books. While those can be helpful in building skill, to achieve more worldly understanding I think you have to read other kinds of books too, including novels, biographies and history books, magazines and newspapers.

For those who prefer visual learning, there are a great many excellent films, both fiction and non-fiction, that serve to open eyes and provoke thought. These provide insight into human nature, trends, and patterns of behaviour. With this knowledge it is possible to rise above the parapet of insular thinking, expand both your personal horizons and your ability to help others move past their perceived limitations.

2. HONOUR DIVERSITY

We are creatures of habit. We like structure. We are fond of our opinions and our biases. And yet, there is much to learn from seeking to understand other perspectives and from being interested in ideas and practices that are foreign to us. Those who hold differing opinions and beliefs have something to teach us. And yet, so often we avoid them or try to change them into something that seems more acceptable to us.

There was a lot written about Steve Jobs in the wake of his untimely death. From all accounts, he was a genius, something of a rebel, a free soul, and a person who didn't only think outside the box but simply chose not to acknowledge the existence of a box in the first place. Apparently, he could also be a very difficult human being: cantankerous, demanding and unapologetic. Yet, we revere him.

 Steve Jobs was the greatest inventor since Thomas Edison. He put the world at our fingertips.

STEVEN SPIELBERG

That's a compelling legacy. It provides an equally compelling reason to treat difference as an asset.

We are each different from the other and not everyone considered *different* is going to be a genius. However, many organizations perpetuate cultures that expect us all to be the same. So no matter where you are in the leadership hierarchy, take the opportunity to honour the jazz of leadership by making room for the ideas and contribution of those whose experience and viewpoints challenge you. You may have to work a little harder but chances are it will help you open doors to things you may not have considered before.

3. Hire People Whose Experience is Deeper and Richer Than the Content of Their Resumes

There was a time when I did a lot of recruiting for the bank. The applicants were largely comprised of newly-minted university graduates, hoping to launch themselves into the business world by passing *Go* and going directly to a management position.

One of those applicants stands out in my memory. I'll call him Michael.

Michael seemed pleasant, presenting himself as confident and eager. When I met him in reception, I offered my hand in greeting and he pumped it up and down so many times I expected to spout water. Nonetheless, I took his enthusiasm as a positive omen and proceeded to the interview room with the anticipation that this was going to be a good interview. However, things didn't go quite as I expected.

Michael sat down in the chair offered, leaned back, slung his right arm over the back of the chair and proceeded to tip it onto its back legs while maintaining his balance with his feet. When comfortably settled, he looked pointedly at me and said, "I have an MBA. What are you going to do for me?"

It took me a few seconds to recover from the impact of that statement. However, my response went something like this.

"Well Michael, I appreciate how hard you must have worked to earn your degree. It says a lot about your ability to focus, and the personal discipline you employed to successfully navigate such a difficult program. What it doesn't tell me about is your ability to apply this learning to a real management role in this organization. So let's explore that, shall we?"

Michael was not pleased. It seemed people were coming out of universities with MBAs expecting, and getting, fast-track management jobs because the assumption was they knew more about management than most. In a number of ways that was true. In Michael's case, what seemed to be lacking was the skill that can only come from life experience.

Having an MBA was a great start, but how had Michael worked through the program? Did he finance it himself? If so, how? Did his parents pay for his education? Had he done any travelling since graduating? If so, where did he go? What did he learn? What about his hobbies and interests? I wanted to know more about the three-dimensional Michael than the one that presented himself simply with the letters MBA emblazoned on his forehead.

I suspect there are organizations that seek solely to hire those whose academic credentials will meet, or even exceed, job requirements. They want people who can hit the ground running, so to speak. While this certainly has to hold weight in hiring decisions, in my observation, those who bring rich life experience to the table may need more orientation and training than the hit-the-ground-running guy but often prove to be better decision-makers and problem-solvers.

How Much Are You Willing to Risk?

Lurking in the shadows of risk is always the prospect of failure. Failure is one of those things we learn to fear for a whole host of reasons, not the least of which is losing something we value or hope to gain. We know that great risk can result in great success... and also failure. Intuitively, we know too that a decision to risk nothing often results in our being left behind. Or worse. And that's another kind of failure.

Consider the plight of the Barnacle goose. Barnacle geese are native to the islands of the North Atlantic, particularly Northeastern Greenland. Normally, they spend their time at sea level where they feed on grass. However when it's time to lay eggs, they build their nests high up on the rocky cliffs above to protect their young from predators. There they are safe and the goslings are allowed to hatch without interference. However, there comes a time when the newly formed family has to make a move. It involves enormous risk but is necessary for their survival because while it is safe to nest on a rock 400 feet up, there is no food up there for them to eat.

This is what I witnessed as I watched an episode of BBC Earth hosted by Sir David Attenborough.

The adult male goose goes first. He spreads his wings and flies to the foot of the cliff, signalling to his mate that it is time. The adult female follows him, and from the earth below, she calls to her babies. The goslings have not yet learned to fly and so they must take the greatest risk of all.

One by one, they each take a leap of faith. They hurl themselves out of the nest into thin air in the hope they will make it to the bottom without injury. Each one executes its leap differently. Some jump from the front of the nest and extend themselves out beyond the rocks as far as possible. Others leap from the back of the nest. Still others fall as if by accident, much too close to the jagged face of the cliff. At some point each gosling hits the rock on the way down. If they strike their bellies, their chances of survival are much greater than if they should hit their heads. It is an eerie sound, the sound of chicks making contact with the hard, cold surface of the rock. It's a kind of squeak that ironically made the gooseflesh rise up on the back of this observer's neck.

When all is done, the parents take inventory of their brood. Three out of five have survived. Apart from being a little dazed, they make haste to join their parents in the quest for a well-earned meal.

You know of course that just being alive is a risk. This story illustrates that in nature this is especially true. In leadership, risk can be more measured, tempered with critical thought. And yet, just like the goslings, it can also ask for leaps of faith. The goslings hurled themselves out of the safety of their nest because they trusted and believed in their mother.

In organizations, people must also have something in which to trust and believe before they can take their leap of faith. They need to be clear about the direction they are headed. They need to be clear about shared goals. They need to be able to place their trust in those who lead them.

As a leader, your task is not only to help others believe in you, but to help them believe in themselves. When you have accomplished this, the general appetite for considered risk and leaps of faith will be that much greater.

So, what is leadership? It is a choice we make rather than something bestowed on us from on high. It is a science and an art. It is a way of being that guides the way of doing. And, it is less symphony and more jazz.

No matter where we sit in the hierarchy of our respective organizations, when we choose leadership, we view the prospect of our work and our lives differently. We look for possibilities and purpose that go beyond servicing our individual needs and ambitions. We experience an expansion in thought and action that feeds growth for ourselves and those we guide.

When you choose leadership from your place in the middle, you choose a place of learning and opportunity to influence in more than one way. In fact, you have a 360-degree view of the landscape and a chance to influence positive growth in every direction.

THINK ABOUT IT

Q. Did you choose leadership or did it choose you? In other words, did you enthusiastically put your hand up for it or were you drafted? Do you think it makes a difference? If so, how?

Q. What was the first thing you learned about being a leader that you hadn't considered before? How might that knowledge be useful to you now?

Q. How do you push out the boundaries of your own understanding to grow both as a leader and a person? Who can help you with that? How might you get more out of it?

Q. So, you might not be willing to jump off a cliff, like the Barnacle goose, but what is your risk tolerance? As a leader, how might you benefit from examining and adjusting your approach to risk-taking?

Q. As a leader, when was the last time you made an assumption about one or more of those who follow you? How did that work out for you?

NOTES

2

CHANGING THE NARRATIVE

While there is opportunity for leaders in the middle to expand and grow, you may not be seeing it yet. There are things getting in the way, maybe old recordings that play in your head, clouding your thoughts about what might be possible, *if only…*

Three such recordings come to mind for me. One is the seemingly constant conversation about whether you are a leader or a manager. The second is the notion that in order to be a good leader you have to have charisma, or at least some magic drawing power that causes people to hang on your every word. (I exaggerate a little, I know.) And thirdly, there is the idea that you cannot have power without authority.

If these things ring a bell with you, maybe together we can shake off the cobwebs and shift your perspective enough to see what's possible for you. That's what this chapter is about.

Leadership versus Management

Having lived this long, (however long *this* is), you might agree that life is made up of a series of beginnings… and endings. It's not difficult to remember the firsts or the lasts of anything significant that happens to us. They seem to define the chapters in our life's story. We underline them, fill in the details and refer to them from time to time because with each beginning and each ending, there are lessons to be learned.

One memorable beginning would be the first time someone put you in charge of a group of others and by implication, added *leadership* to your list of responsibilities. You may not have recognized the subtleness of the slide from follower to leader. The word *leadership* may not even have come up. Indeed I expect the word *management* was used more often.

When I became an assistant manager, there was no particular attention paid to leadership. Leadership was a word reserved for those who operated in the rarified air of the C-Suite. The idea of leadership being something required of a middle manager was foreign. I was a manager, not a leader. I managed. That was my job. On top of that, there was no apparent thought given to whether I had the skill necessary to lead others, only to whether I was capable of meeting deadlines, managing (not leading) the people, and getting the work done.

While many companies are more enlightened than that, remnants of the old remain. Somewhat like ghosts in the attic amid the old pictures, toys, and memorabilia of the past, the idea that middle managers only manage continues to lurk. I know because entering the search term, "leader versus manager" produced 1.5 billion results.

The notion that people can be slotted into one of two categories and labeled either leader or manager is, to me, unproductive. After all, the activities of a designated person-in-charge involve both leadership *and* management. So if you are a middle manager in charge of a group of others and doing only one of those things, you are also doing only half of your job. I don't mean to be harsh. And, for the record, I am betting that much of your work, while possibly classified as management, involves much more leadership than you might be given credit for.

The common view is that management is less than sexy, boring, and perhaps even repressive in some way. We shine our light on leadership because we hold visions in our heads of the leader as some kind of hero. We do it because the hero breaks rules, takes risks, and bestows freedom where once there was only containment. So when the "Are you a leader or a manager?" question comes up, nobody wants to choose *manager*. That's for people with no imagination. People who spend their time enforcing rules and keeping everyone from living up to their potential.

Rubbish.

It doesn't matter what you're called in the official sense. Whether it's supervisor, manager, senior manager, team leader or grand poobah twice removed, as long as you have responsibility for the work of a group of others, both leadership and management is required of you.

If you're not sure when to do what, a simple rule of thumb is: manage things, lead people. In other words, manage processes, plans, time, expectations, files, and your own behaviour.

The rest is trickier. It involves guiding, coaching, setting expectations, encouraging, challenging, and above all, through your influence, inspiring others to give their best work to the achievement of your shared goals. That's the leadership part. And yes, that may be where you, as leader of people, will take risks, break rules that don't make sense and let go of control enough to give wings to new ideas. That's possibly the harder part but it is also possibly the best part.

Charismatic Leaders versus Everybody Else

Some might think in order to accomplish the leadership part you need that elusive thing called charisma, or at least some natural leadership ability.

Charisma seems to be something we admire in others and wish we had more of in ourselves. It has drawing power. When we see it in leaders, that compelling charm that inspires us to listen and follow and emulate, it is easy to envy the apparent ease with which the charismatic spin their magic.

Charismatic leaders also paint the picture of the leader as hero. These are people whose very presence suggests they can take care of us, cure our ills, and make change possible without pain. Maybe they're the saviour we have long sought.

In reality, no one can do all of this single-handedly, if at all. Charisma may deliver the promise of change, growth, fulfillment, and even wealth, but on its own it will fail in the execution department. Execution requires astute management and a different kind of leadership.

Having said that, let's face it. Having charisma can be very handy. Can we develop it? I'm not sure. The word itself comes from the Greek meaning gift. We know that each of us has gifts. Not everyone possesses that particular one.

Nonetheless, I can't help but feel that what draws us to the charismatic type is not unlike what inspires us to follow leaders with less, um, pizzazz. So from that perspective I think it possible to develop, and use, some of the skills associated with the charismatic personality.

Here are three traits associated with the charismatic leader:

- excellent communication skills
- self-awareness
- intense focus

These and other elements can indeed be developed, even among those of us who have had what Jim Collins describes as a "charisma bypass" because, as he says, charisma is a personality trait[1]. And leadership is not about personality.

Charisma, on its own, tends to burn bright and then burn out. It has a dark side too. Adolph Hitler had it[2]. So did The Reverend Jim Jones[3] and Osama bin Laden[4]. All three have had a disastrous impact on humankind. Masses of people, at one time or another, have viewed them with awe, often blindly doing their bidding. These leaders are people who fed on the hope and despair of others to their own advantage and for their own glorification. Charisma gave them that opportunity.

So if we strive for anything in leadership, let's work to transform rather than transfix. Transformational leadership[5] contains an element of charisma but is grounded in a set of high ideals, a solid work ethic and the expectation that all people have the capability to raise themselves up through their own hard work to reach higher ground.

Those who work to transform may share some charismatic traits, but they differ in these important areas.

THEY FOCUS ON A PURPOSE AND VISION GREATER THAN THEMSELVES. Their work is not about them but about something beyond them that serves a greater good.

THEY ENGAGE OTHERS IN MAKING THE VISION THEIR OWN. This comes from the belief that a shared purpose and vision makes the necessity for change clearer and the work it takes to achieve it, more meaningful.

THEY VALUE LEARNING, CREATIVITY, AND PERSONAL GROWTH. Transformational leaders encourage people to challenge what has always been and to explore new possibilities with enthusiasm and without fear.

THEY CARRY LESS MYSTIQUE AND MORE TRANSPARENCY. To involve everyone in fulfilling the organizational purpose demands a kind of openness that doesn't exist in a company whose leader relies solely on the strength of his or her personality to lead. Mystique may be kind of sexy but it gets in the way of getting the job done.

While we are not all favoured with charisma, we do each have the opportunity to develop drawing power by building leadership skill; nurturing relationships; being open to learning; focusing on something beyond ourselves; and mustering the courage to challenge and change things. If we can do all that, who needs charisma?

To me, it comes down to one thing. As a leader, in the middle or otherwise, if you care about the work, and particularly about the people who are doing it, the rest can be learned.

Power versus Authority

Some people believe the words *power* and *authority* are synonymous. I'm more inclined to believe that authority and power, while linked, are two different things.

For instance, it is possible for you to have authority without power if you are a newly appointed manager. People reporting to you will likely have little or no experience with you as a leader. As such, they may be reticent to follow your directives. Your authority only carries real power when you have earned their trust and respect and when they can see merit in the direction you want to take them. In short, the power kicks in when they give it to you.

Conversely, it is possible to have power without authority when, as a well-informed, competent, and reliable team member, people seek out your advice and guidance. While you may not have the authority to make certain decisions on your own, you influence other team members who have come to respect your judgment and are eager to follow your lead.

Of course the challenge is to optimize the authority we are given by persuading others to not only believe it is well placed, but also to endorse and respect it. When we have accomplished that, then words like power and authority become more easily interchangeable.

Here is how you can close the gap between authority and power.

Be Yourself

Some people believe that when they are awarded the mantle of authority, they must behave in a certain authoritative way. However, authority has no particular personality trait. It is simply a mechanism provided to some people that expedites decision-making and getting things done. When you represent yourself honestly, people are more likely to accept and trust you. And that's where the power lies.

Listen and Learn

The decisions you make are only as good as the information on which you base them. Your authority gives you permission to make decisions. The power behind the authority lies in the willingness of the leader to listen, learn and make informed decisions.

Roll Up Your Sleeves and Join In

There are times when the leader becomes the servant. This is when everyone is clear about what must be accomplished and you, as leader, do whatever you can to support the process. You may certainly have the authority to command work be done without participating yourself. However, sometimes rolling up the sleeves to help is just what is needed to inject enthusiasm into the mix and create positive working relationships. And that can be pretty powerful.

Recognize and Reward Good Work

If you want to put power behind your authority, the good work of others must never go unrecognized. As humans, we all need to know that we, and our efforts, are appreciated. And, in the workplace, recognition is very much valued when it comes from a person in authority and is offered with sincerity. Most of us, when given such recognition, are eager to do more and to do it happily. That's where the power comes from.

As a leader, you will have a certain level of authority for making decisions and organizing the work in a way that best suits your purpose. This authority will be limited by the dictates of your organization. Power and influence, on the other hand, come from the respect and credibility you earn, and the trust you build in your relationships with others at all levels of the organization. You could say, the possibility for this is limitless, only restricted by the confines of your personal choice. From this perspective, it really doesn't matter what your title is or where you are in the organizational pecking order.

Leadership versus management, charisma versus everybody else, and power versus authority are the most common old recordings that you may find buzzing around your head like mosquitoes on a hot summer night. The point is, if something gets in the way of your ability to expand your capacity to lead, it's worth challenging. And it's worth changing the way you think and talk about it.

THINK ABOUT IT

Q. How is your view of leadership and management shaping your approach and the outcomes you achieve? For an optimal experience, what might you want to start doing? What might you want to stop doing? What's working that you want to keep?

Q. If you're like me and seem to have undergone a *charisma bypass* somewhere along the way, you might now understand charisma as a gift to some, but not all. What are your gifts if charisma isn't one of them? How do you use them to help those you lead engage in the work and get things done? How might you build on the gifts you already have for even better outcomes?

Q. In your experience, can you remember having authority without power? Why do you think that was? How did it make you feel? What did you do about it?

Q. Conversely, can you think of a time when you had power but little or no authority? What were the circumstances? What did you do with the power given to you? How did it work out for you?

Q. How could the knowledge that power and authority are not always aligned change the way you approach your work and the people in your life? What would be different?

NOTES

3

LEADING ON PURPOSE

I n a world of unrelenting change, your choice to lead can be difficult. You live and work in a sea of uncertainty. Because of that, you need to find an anchor, something to reassure you that you're on the right path. I believe that something is called *purpose.*

In this chapter, we will make the distinction between working for a purpose and working for results because, while related, they're not really the same. We'll talk about the differences between values, purpose, mission, and vision to help you figure out how each of these things can serve you from your place in the middle. We'll also discuss the importance of self-awareness as a place to start any purposeful expedition. And finally, we'll talk about how all these things fit with your reality as a middle leader.

Purpose and Shifting Perspective

If you never really thought of leading from the middle as a place of opportunity, you may be re-thinking that position now. The question is, how will you start to convert that new thinking into something tangible for you and those you lead?

I expect you see some obstacles. Perhaps your working environment seems limiting when it comes to introducing new ideas. Maybe your organization places a lot of emphasis on the chain of command making you, as leader-in-the-middle, something of an upstart who doesn't know your place. It's not uncommon.

The good news is that many traditional organizations are in transition from an old model where power and authority are bestowed on just a few, to a newer more enlightened and collaborative one. It is necessary, in the age of technology, to create flexible systems and practices that push decision-making away from the few at the top, down, and out through the organization so that response time can keep up with customer demand for instant gratification.

The not-so-good news is this shift in culture and practice is painful. And so, like a stretched elastic band, the old way tentatively ventures to embrace the new, only to snap back sharply at the first sign of trouble.

Finding purpose in your work and helping others do the same is the essence of good leadership. The hard part is in the finding.

It's difficult because we often confuse *purpose* with *desired results* or *outcomes*.

As a case in point, in 1988, I moved to Vancouver to take up a new role as a Human Resources Consultant. As I was very new to the city and to the corporate banking environment, it was agreed that I should go on a road trip to visit various banking centres and meet with as many employees as possible. It was an orientation for me and provided a chance for everyone else to give me the "once over." After all, I'd come from Toronto.

Apparently, the perspective of most Vancouver bankers was that those coming from Toronto usually brought with them an attitude of superiority. It's an odd rivalry of sorts, between Canada's largest city (Toronto) and its third largest (Vancouver), with Torontonians viewing Vancouverites as provincial-minded hippies with an unhealthy focus on physical fitness and Vancouverites viewing Torontonians as self-centred know-it-alls with an unhealthy focus on work. So in spite of having left my self-importance packed away in some obscure place that even I couldn't find, it seemed I was not to be trusted.

On one occasion, I was to talk with a number of corporate account managers. My goal was to get to know them as individuals, to learn about their ambitions, their challenges, and how we might better support their efforts.

Ron was the first person I met. He struck quite an imposing figure, with a hawkish expression and a hairline well back from his forehead. Curiously, what hair remained stood sentry over the bald place as if in a constant state of alarm.

On this day, Ron loomed large in the doorway. Before entering the room, he paused to take the measure of me. Then, in what seemed like two giant strides, he was standing in front of me, pulling his chair uncomfortably close to mine. He sat down heavily, leaned forward until we were almost nose-to-nose and stared sharply into my face. Then he said, "I make money for the bank. What do you do?"

Aside from the obvious attempt to intimidate me, Ron's question was meant to suggest that as a person who made no direct contribution to the bottom line, I was an expense to the organization and therefore a liability.

This was not an unfamiliar perspective to take, especially in such a large traditional organization. But at the time, I couldn't help but think there was something gravely missing from this outlook. In fact, it occurred to me that *making money for the bank*, while an admirable outcome, did not tell me anything about what Ron saw as his purpose.

If I'm honest, I like money as well as the next person. But the purpose of most jobs, most businesses, and even most lives is not principally about money. It is more likely something else, a purpose that has to do with filling a need or being of service in some way. Making money is only one of the rewards that come from that.

As an example, Zappos.com is in the business of delivering happiness. That's its purpose, why it exists. And, it must do a very good job of fulfilling its purpose because this company produces more than $2 billion in revenue each year.

Okay. So the lines between purpose, its cousins vision, mission, and values can get pretty blurry. It's made even more confusing when companies themselves mix them up or spend money developing them only to frame them, hang them on the wall, and do precious little else with them after that. To be fair, perhaps this was Ron's dilemma. His organization doesn't have a purpose statement, but included in its vision is the intent to "put the client at the centre of all we do."

Ron appeared to make little or no connection to this. Let's imagine what could have been possible if he had chosen to give more serious consideration to the notion of putting clients at the centre of all he did. Perhaps he might have seen his purpose as *delivering solid financial solutions that lead to growth and prosperity for all,* instead of *making money for the bank.*

This simple shift in perspective might very well have made a difference in the way Ron approached his work and colleagues. And me. Maybe he would even have viewed the work of those in roles other than his own as a vital part of fulfilling a purpose with deeper and wider implications. Who knows?

Values, Purpose, Mission, Vision

Not all organizations have a formal and stated purpose, although most have developed vision, mission, and values statements meant to shape the organizational culture and guide its strategy. Often, these terms are used interchangeably even though they mean different things. Let's make some distinctions between them.

(To do this I'm going to use examples that may or may not accurately reflect the current statements of each company. These examples are as reported in third party articles located in the course of my research and are for illustrative purposes only.)

VALUES STATEMENTS ADDRESS THE QUESTION: WHAT MATTERS TO US?

At its heart, a values statement expresses the kind of ethos a company supports and encourages. It defines its character and its culture. A good set of core values can become a useful instrument for hiring and decision-making if established and used in a way that is both clear and actionable.

Example:

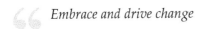

Embrace and drive change

ZAPPOS.COM

This values statement urges action but also subtly infers that the bedrock of embracing and driving change is... courage.

PURPOSE STATEMENTS ANSWER THE QUESTION: WHY DO WE EXIST?
They go beyond the confines of the organizational structure to include the wider community. They express a company's philosophy and its intent to positively affect the lives of those it serves.
Example:

At Tangerine, we're committed to helping Canadians live better lives. It's why we come in to work each and every day. And it's our purpose for delivering forward banking to Canadians.

TANGERINE BANK

MISSION STATEMENTS ANSWER THE QUESTION: WHAT DO WE DO?
Mission statements provide a structure within which to operate. A mission statement can be tightly focussed and include information about products, customers and target markets.
Example:

To deliver information on the people, ideas and technologies changing the world to our community of affluent business decision makers.

FORBES

Other mission statements will be shorter and just as effective, like this one:

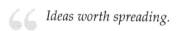

Ideas worth spreading.

TED

Vision statements answer the question: what will we look like in the future?

They provide something to strive for that doesn't currently exist. They are also dynamic and can change over time, as new information, new technology, or new events give cause to re-imagine what the future holds. Vision statements don't have be wordy or fancy. They do need to paint a picture of the future.

Example:

A world without Alzheimer's disease.

ALZHEIMER'S ASSOCIATION

In short, understanding your values, purpose, mission, and vision will provide focus and structure to everything you do. Whether at a very high level of an organization or somewhere in the middle of it, the questions and their answers will apply. What matters to you (values)? Why do you exist (purpose)? What do you do (mission)? What does your future look like (vision)?

So yes, knowing your values and purpose and all that sounds pretty good. But where do you start?

Establishing Your Own Values, Purpose, Mission, and Vision

So we've made distinctions between values, purpose, mission, and vision (v/p/m/v) from an organizational perspective but we haven't yet considered how these definitions fit for you. As a leader in the middle, you may believe you have little or no control over the establishment of these seemingly lofty pursuits. To some extent this may be true, if we're talking about the v/p/m/v for your organization. However, you do have control over:

- how you interpret those statements
- how you go about fulfilling the messages they send
- how you think about and develop your own personal
  v/p/m/v

You may also have some degree of control over developing or articulating the v/p/m/v for your section, area, or team.

If you're unsure of your company's purpose or its vision for the future, getting some clarity about this would be a good place to start. If you do have clarity but don't see how your role and the roles of those you lead fit into the overall picture, there is an opportunity here to carve out a more finely focussed purpose and vision that substantiates your team's value to the organization.

Doing so asks you to be bold. It also allows you the potential to push out the boundaries of your influence by demonstrating what's possible when you work toward fulfilling a clearly stated purpose. You will, of course, be judged by your results. But no matter what position you lead from in your organization, if you take the time to do the work associated with v/p/m/v, you will be in a better place to:

- align your work with that of the rest of your organization
- influence other leaders and decision makers in determining
  your company's strategies and tactics
- identify opportunities to articulate both the contribution you
  make and the importance of your role and the roles of those
  you lead in fulfilling the organizational purpose

Doing this work takes time. Perhaps it's time you feel you don't have. However, once done, it will provide clarity of direction and purpose where once there may have been uncertainty. It will help you build the confidence you need to make important decisions, set priorities, and challenge the status quo.

It All Begins with Self-Awareness

Knowing yourself deeply and being able to say what matters to you will eventually allow you to clear the cobwebs away from self and connect to something larger.

Basically, self-awareness is about knowing your own strengths, weaknesses, behaviours, and attitudes well enough to understand your impact on those around you. It will also help you to find answers to the questions that will connect you to your values, purpose, mission, and vision. Peter Senge, renowned thought leader and author of *The Fifth Discipline*, calls this self-awareness personal mastery.

Practically speaking, there are instruments available on the internet to get you started. These tools are designed to help you confirm not only what you might already know about yourself but also uncover some things you don't know. However you do it, the key to successful personal mastery is to be curious, ask questions about how others experience you, either formally or informally, and purposefully observe your own impact when you work with them.

To gain even more information, it is sometimes helpful to engage a trusted ally who will provide you with another perspective on the influence you have on others.

Here's a story to illustrate what I mean.

Once upon a time, there was a boss called Boss who was very sure of himself. Boss was strong and competent. He had built some admirable relationships with his peers and was well-liked by his customers and the community at large. But he was also puzzled.

Boss was puzzled because it seemed, to him anyway, that every time he walked into the same room as his employees, the conversation went from lively to subdued and restrained. And, when a question came up during meetings with his team, they all looked at him before attempting to answer. Similarly, when they talked about problems, the team members looked his way before, or while, giving their opinions.

On the one hand, Boss kind of liked it. It made him feel, well, in control and more than a little powerful. On the other hand, he found it irritating and unproductive. Surely these people were fully capable of drawing conclusions and deciding on courses of action without waiting for his blessing all the time. Did he have to do everything? What was wrong with them?

Then one day, a Brave Soul approached Boss and said, "You know, you can be pretty intimidating sometimes."

Boss looked at Brave Soul with eyes so hard and blue they seemed cold enough to freeze mercury.

Boss said, "What? What do you mean? All I did was walk into the room and sit down!"

Slightly shaken but undaunted, Brave Soul went on. "Well," she said, "it's not just that you walked into the room but how you did it."

"Okay," Boss said. "Now that really is ridiculous. How could that possibly make me intimidating? I'm interested in what people have to say. I want some healthy discussion and debate about the issues we face. I need people to be fully present when we meet so we can work together and get things done. Don't they get that?"

Brave Soul replied, "I'm pretty sure that's what they want too. But the effect your body language and behaviour has on the team makes it difficult for them to participate."

Unconvinced but intrigued, Boss encouraged Brave Soul to tell him more.

"Well, when you came into the room this morning, you didn't acknowledge anyone. You probably had a lot on your mind and so you were frowning too. You walked straight to your chair at the head of the table and sat down without looking at anyone. You looked at your watch instead. You opened your book, peered over your glasses at the assembled group and said, 'Okay, let's get to it. We have a lot to do and I've got another meeting after this.' After that, it seemed to the team that the goal of the meeting changed from one that involved sharing ideas and making productive decisions to coming up with enough right answers to keep you from getting too impatient and ensuring that you got away in time to get to your next meeting."

"That's not what I intended at all!" said Boss. Inside, Boss started to realize he underestimated his effect on people.

As though she could read Boss's mind instead of just his body language, Brave Soul smiled and said, "I don't think any of us knows how we affect others unless we take some time to think about it and ask. Sometimes how we are can get in the way of things. That's all. Just thought you should know."

As Brave Soul walked away, Boss made a mental note. He had learned something today about himself. He didn't like it, but if what Brave Soul had said were true, it would certainly explain the behaviour he saw and felt in others.

So, Boss wondered what he could do differently to become more aware of his impact without pretending to be someone other than himself. Here's what he came up with:

I will make an effort to become aware of the clues that people are sending me when we are in each other's company. It seems reasonable that if people can pick up and act on clues from my body language and behaviour, I can pick up clues about how I affect them by paying better attention when we're together.

When in doubt about my impact on others, I will ask someone I trust to tell me the truth. I get that I will not always be able to see myself as others see me. So, I will ask someone like Brave Soul to watch me from time to time and let me know how I'm doing.

I will be conscious of my moods and do my best to manage them in a way that doesn't negatively affect those around me. I realize that when I'm deep in thought or worried about something, it isn't difficult to convey it through my body language to those around me. So, from now on I must either explain myself or be disciplined enough to convey a more open posture.

Commitment to these three actions proved to be a great help to Boss. Did he make a miraculous transformation? No, not really. That would probably be too much to ask. However, Brave Soul noticed that Boss would, from time to time, catch himself in his old ways and, without prompting, adjust his behaviour accordingly.

And that, my friend, is the earmark of self-awareness. The pursuit of it may seem like a lot of work and for some it will be tedious work at that. However, once you get a firm grip on who you are and what matters to you, you will be able to shift your focus away from yourself and toward the pursuit of your purpose.

In fact, one of the best things about being a leader in the middle is you have the unique opportunity to influence down the organization as well as up and sideways. If you lead from a solid understanding of your-self and your values, purpose, mission, and vision, your chances of building and keeping credibility as a leader and affecting change in your organization will be that much greater.   And that's what leading on purpose is all about.

THINK ABOUT IT

Leading on purpose is not just about leading in an organizational capacity. It's also about leading a life.

Q. Think of yourself as a company of one with an employee of one... you. What matters to you? What is your purpose? What do you do to fulfil it? When you close your eyes and imagine your future, what do you see?

Q. How does all of that fit with your current reality as a leader? As a person? If you were to feel the need to change something, what might that be?

Q. How self-aware do you think you are? How do you know? What do you need to work on to increase your self-awareness? Who might your Brave Soul be?

NOTES

SECTION II: COMMUNICATION

4

A FLY IN THE OINTMENT OF PROGRESS

On the surface, communicating with one another should be simple. As humans, we're issued ears for hearing, mouths for speaking, and fingers for writing (or texting). We each have a brain with which to think and make all those other parts work. However, like most tools, we have to learn to make the most efficient use of them. This is usually where the trouble starts. The mouth kicks in before the brain engages. The ears process the sound waves but we fail to listen. The prose strikes a wrong chord or conveys a message that is contrary to its intent. Before you know it, there is misunderstanding, missed opportunity, and misconnection everywhere.

In this chapter we'll discuss the myth of *lack of communication*. We'll look at some of the pitfalls that get in the way of effective communication and what you can do to steer clear. I'll introduce some things for you to think about with respect to linguistic and cultural differences, and a new way to think about bias. I'll ask you to see if you see yourself in a few examples of self-indulgent communication, and finally we'll talk about how language is evolving to shape communication in the workplace.

Lack of Communication

Good leadership without good communication skill is not possible. Being able to convey clear messages regardless of the conveyance and to accurately decipher incoming messages is the bedrock from which you build your reputation as a leader. So, it's a big hairy deal. Even the most seasoned leader needs to pay attention and learn how to improve how they communicate. I know because when I worked with bank executives, this was an ongoing struggle.

These bank executives were all very successful people with a wide range of talents, skills, and personalities. You'd expect them to be good at this stuff. However, when faced with a problem that involved people (and what problem doesn't?) they would invariably say, "It's a lack of communication."

Lack of communication was a throwaway remark that seemed to come wrapped in hope that just saying it would resolve the problem. Of course it didn't. And they knew it didn't. But maybe they just didn't know where to start. These were bankers whose work, while complex and often intricate, was black and white in nature. Communication has many shades of grey.

Blaming problems in the workplace on lack of communication suggests that communication in organizations doesn't exist, or that there's not enough of it. It does. And there is. It just has a nasty habit of being ineffective and dysfunctional.

Effective Communication

Communication is effective when you tell me something and I understand it the way you meant it.

That doesn't sound too complicated. Yet, you'll know from painful experience it is easier to say than to do. Even if you try to simplify communication processes, barriers can sabotage the message and render it ineffective by the time it gets to its intended recipient. Here are some major obstacles to watch for and some suggestions as to what to do about them.

. . .

Hearing versus Listening

Listening is an art form. Generally, human beings are not very good at it. It requires time and concentration. For example, if I am nodding and looking at you while you're speaking, but at the same time I'm thinking about what I'm going to say next, I'm not really listening. If, in that exchange, you are doing the same thing, the words serve only as a game of verbal badminton with the message being a meaningless shuttlecock batted hopelessly back and forth until it loses momentum altogether.

To really listen, you must suspend your ego, opinions, and thoughts to make room for and pay attention to someone else's. This involves asking questions for clarification and repeating what you hear to ensure the message you get matches the message being delivered. You don't have to agree with what is being said. But listening, really listening, asks you to give some time over to learning about the views and opinions of others in such a way that you become informed enough to either stick with your current view or reassess.

Assumptions

 Assume and you make an ass out of you and me.

UNKNOWN

Making assumptions about what other people think, know, or understand can send a well-intended message off the rails. For instance, you may assume that because people are nodding while you speak, they understand and agree with what you are saying. Similarly, if you invite questions after making a presentation and you get none, it would be easy to assume there are none. But it might also be possible that no one understood your message in the first place. Or, it could be that no one is willing to risk the potential embarrassment of being the only one who doesn't agree with or understand your message. Perhaps they don't know what to ask. Whatever the reason, to assume that your message

essfully received because it has been met with silence
stake.

act the natural tendency to make assumptions, it might
on the basis that all of your assumptions, no matter what
they are, could be false. As such, it would make sense to make your
assumptions known to others just to check their validity before
launching yourself off in the wrong direction.

LINGUISTIC DIFFERENCES

Variance in expression or colloquialism is common even among those
who speak the same language.

When my parents brought our family to Canada from England, there
were a lot of expressions we used that were interpreted differently in our
new country. This once placed my mother in an embarrassing situation
when one day she was sitting around a table with her co-workers
discussing the time they each got up in the morning to get ready for
work. When it came to Mum's turn to speak she said, "My husband
knocks me up every morning at seven thirty."

It was only after the laughter had died down that someone explained
to her the North American meaning associated with being knocked up.
(If you're from elsewhere, it means to *make pregnant*.) Mum had a good
laugh at herself and also remembered the lesson that even though she
spoke English, the nuances of North American vernacular could distort
her meaning if she didn't pay closer attention to her choices of
expression.

Business speak is in a similar vein. This is one of the biggest reasons
understanding gets lost (a.k.a. a lack of communication) in the workplace. For some reason, when we walk into the office, our ability to speak
plainly walks out.

Speaking and writing plainly does not suggest lack of intelligence or
knowledge. Quite the opposite. Someone who is able to get a clear
message across—with minimal head scratching on the part of the recipient—is very clever indeed.

So the next time you are tempted to say something like, "Going
forward we will dialogue about the deliverables, ensure that we have

buy-in from all stakeholders and then circle back to close the loop on the project," please stop yourself. Perhaps instead say, "From now on, let's talk more about what we have to produce, make sure all those affected by what we are doing agree, and then meet again to talk about how we can finish the project."

If you strive to simplify your language and minimize your use of slang, idioms, and jargon, more people will understand you more quickly, easily, and more often. Then you can get more done.

CULTURAL DIFFERENCES

Cultural differences are made up of the attitudes and beliefs that come from our personal environment and experience. As such, two people could get the same message but interpret it in two entirely different ways simply because they have different frames of reference.

If you want people to receive and understand your message the way you mean it to be understood, you must:

- pay particular attention to the culture of your audience
- seek to understand where there may be differences in interpretation
- fashion your message in a way that says what you mean and takes those differences into account

BIASES

We all have them. Bias is, after all, shaped by our experiences and who we are. However, bias becomes a problem in communicating effectively when we consciously or subconsciously choose to speak only to those who are more likely to understand and agree with us. It's natural. And yet, in leadership, it is also important to extend the reach of your message to include those whose own biases do not align with your own.

In your workplace, for instance, I'd imagine there are people from more than one generation. Each generation has its view of the world. For example, baby boomers live to work, while Millennials work to live.

Those differing perspectives bring differing biases. Each generation also has its challenges. Your challenge is to find a way to reach and engage everyone despite the difference in their preferences and expectations. So what do you do?

Acknowledge your own biases first because these are going to shape your message from the start. Then look through the lens of those who are least likely to align with your views. Maybe test your message with a few people to see how it lands, and then adjust it with a view to increasing the possibility of achieving deeper and wider understanding among your target audience. You may not get agreement. After all, understanding and agreement are two different things. However, the greater the common understanding the more accurate and meaningful your conversations will be. Agreement, compromise, or (even better) solutions and ideas can flow from that if you start your deliberations on similar ground.

Self-Indulgent Communication

Communicating with others is kind of like a dance. It has its own rhythm. There is a time to speak, a time to listen, and there is also a time to keep quiet. Knowing when to do what often makes the difference between achieving a graceful dance and stepping on your partner's toes.

 Never miss a good chance to shut up.

WILL ROGERS

Rarely do we consider that effective communication also means keeping quiet at times. And yet, nothing can be more effective in reaching understanding than a well-placed pause, a time when we step back and listen, not only to others but also to ourselves.

First though, we have to be able to recognize when we are talking too much and listening too little and, as a result, eroding the depth and importance of our conversations.

So when, you might ask, would that happen to you?

• • •

WHEN YOU'RE ANGRY. Subtext: I'm mad, so I'm going to vent all over you so that *I* can feel better. Anger sometimes compels us to put the mouth in gear before the brain has had time to process what's going on. And that can make an already bad situation worse. Being on the receiving end of someone's flare-up is a sure-fire way to shut down lines of communication altogether.

WHEN YOU'RE TEMPTED TO SAY ANY OLD THING TO FILL A VOID. Subtext: I'm uncomfortable so I'm going to say something because somebody has to! Silence can be cringe-worthy. For instance, in a meeting you put an idea up for discussion, you ask for some thoughts... and nothing happens. You sit and wait for a few seconds. And then you can't stand it any more so you start talking just to punch the silence into submission. The thing is, when the silence is only allowed for a few seconds, you may be missing an opportunity to hear from someone who simply needs a little more time to process the information on the table before sharing an opinion about it. So, tolerating pauses, pregnant or otherwise, could be a very positive discipline to develop.

WHEN YOU'RE CONVINCED OF YOUR *RIGHTNESS*. Subtext: I'm right and I'm going to keep on talking until you agree with me. Sometimes we can fall in love with our own ideas so much that we make no space for the possibility of being wrong. Clinging to a position and arguing its virtues can be great fun but if you are not willing to listen to others' perspectives and soften the edges of your views in the face of new information, you become a roadblock to progress.

WHEN YOU REALIZE YOU DON'T REALLY KNOW WHAT YOU'RE TALKING ABOUT. Subtext: I'm lost but I'll look like a fool if I stop talking now. Every once in a while, I will embark on a line of conversation and then lose the thread of it completely. Instead of stopping to get re-focussed, I will keep talking in the hope that eventually, I'll get to the point. I rather suspect this happens to everyone at some point. When it happens, it's embarrassing. But frankly so is taking people on a meander you didn't intend. As for me, I find it helps to simply stop, mid-ramble, and admit to having no idea where I was going with my line of verbal diarrhea. We all have a laugh about it and then move on to something more productive.

There is a common theme running through the four occasions I've described above. Each is a self-indulgent response. In communication, as in leadership, self-indulgence will get in the way of success every time.

Language

I have always loved language. Admittedly, my facility in it is sadly limited to English, a few French words and phrases, body language, paralanguage and oh yes, a little Pig Latin. Nonetheless, what I love about language is its power to shape ideas, create images, evoke emotion, and give birth to new habits and traditions.

Communication encompasses all we do and all we are—whether or not we recognize it. Over the years, the way we communicate in the workplace has changed, not only with respect to the devices available to us in receiving and conveying messages, but in the language we use as well.

In organizations, language also has the power to determine what matters. For instance, the language of the twentieth century stressed, among other things, the importance of control, competition, individual targets, winning, losing, and results. While many of these words allude to activities that continue to be important, there is other language finding its way onto the twenty-first century landscape that will affect our behaviour and change the way we communicate with each other.

To some, this language is associated with the softer side of life. It has often been derided and dismissed as being too ethereal or without merit in the workplace. But language like this stands a chance of re-shaping what matters and revealing its harder edge as we use it. It stresses the importance of empathy, inclusion, self-awareness, diversity in thought and culture, openness, adaptability, and collaboration.

In so many ways, these words and the language surrounding them, while sounding soft, are a lot harder to live by because they demand time, work, and above all ways of communicating with each other that must consider multiple viewpoints, values, and cultures.

In many ways, this twenty-first century language renders communication more complex. Sometimes you may wonder if it's worth the effort. And yet, to create understanding from your communication with others and ultimately get things done well, you must first understand the people you are communicating with.

Only then can you master effective communication and send messages that are understood the way you meant them.

THINK ABOUT IT

Q. Considering the communication practices in your workplace, what works well?

Q. What isn't working as well as you'd like? Why do think that is?

Q. While improving your entire organizational communication system may be unrealistic, what steps could you personally take to contribute to achieving better understanding between you and your bosses? Your peers? Those you lead?

Q. How often do you find yourself playing *verbal badminton* with someone in your workplace and getting nothing out of the conversation because you're busy thinking about what you're going to say when they finish talking? (It happens to everyone.) What might you do to improve your ability to suspend your thoughts long enough to fully understand what someone is saying to you?

Q. If Will Rogers is right and you should never miss an opportunity to shut up, what benefit do you think doing so would bring you? What might you need to do differently to get to the place where knowing when to keep quiet becomes part of your *muscle memory*?

NOTES

5

TRANSMISSION

 Whatever words we utter should be chosen with care for people will hear them for good or ill.

BUDDHA

A s a leader in the middle, communication can be a multi-tasking nightmare. It could seem that you have no control over the quality or accuracy of available information and to some extent that's true. However, you do have an opportunity to influence the quality of the communication that goes out from you and from those who report to you. You also have control over how you respond to messages that come in to you.

In this chapter we delve into the transmission side of good communication, which involves two main things: creating an environment that supports and encourages the establishment of successful communication practices; and understanding the standards, or values, on which effective communication are most often founded.

First, I'm going to reminisce on the evolution of the transmission of messages because there are things we just don't do anymore. Take elocution lessons, for example.

When I was seven years old, in England, elocution was part of our school curriculum. Of course, that might have been because most of us in the class had a dreadful habit of dropping our "haiches" and committing other such crimes against the English language. What intrigues me today is that someone in her wisdom decided we should learn to speak so that we could also be understood.

What a concept.

Enter Miss Frost, a woman whose demeanour befitted her name, small, grey and wizened, with the ability to freeze one to the core with one look. Miss Frost had us all standing at attention on many an occasion repeating after her, "How now, brown cow," shaping our little mouths, like baby birds, as roundly as we could so the sounds would come out to her satisfaction.

I suspect we did not satisfy Miss Frost, as her temper never seemed to improve nor did our penchant for "haiche" dropping. Nonetheless, I did come to know that words, when pronounced with care, tend to convey a clearer meaning than when we allow them to carelessly careen off the end of our tongues and get hopelessly enmeshed in jargon, saliva, and each other.

And then there's penmanship. There was a time when the only way to communicate in writing was with pen and paper. In school we learned how to shape our letters and write in straight lines and when we received gifts from relatives and friends at Christmas and other important occasions, it was obligatory to sit down and write carefully-crafted notes of thanks. A painful exercise when one is small. But it taught me the importance of acknowledgement and that maintaining good relationships with others requires making an effort to be appreciative and gracious. That hasn't changed.

Now, it is much easier to sit at a computer and send e-mails, or text, or tweet. The ways we can communicate with each other without putting pen to paper are amazingly diverse. I approve wholeheartedly of anything that helps us keep our relationships alive and well.

However, the ability to speak clearly and add a personal touch to our gratitude by actually handwriting a legible note of appreciation once in a while are tools that continue to have great value. They are simple implements of transmission that help create an environment that facilitates comprehension and good will.

Creating an Environment that Nurtures Positive and Effective Communication

There are a few things that can either support or interfere with effective communication. Including the extent to which:

- you encourage or discourage casual conversation in your workplace
- you manage office politics
- you appreciate and practice straight talk

Your approach to each will have an impact on the kind of working environment you create as a leader and also the kind of messages you send out.

Casual Conversation...Something to Talk About

Do you participate in and encourage casual conversation in your workplace? Or, do you choose not to involve yourself in idle talk and discourage those around you from chatting as well? I've met people who think that spending time talking to people about this and that serves little purpose but to waste time.

In my experience, there are definite advantages to encouraging and participating in casual conversations around the office.

As a leader, when you engage in conversation with those you lead, you are giving yourself and your organization an opportunity to know them beyond what you saw on their resumes when you hired them. As leader, it is your job to know what resources you have to work with. The people on your team are resources. Human resources. Having casual conversations with the people around you reveals more about their talents, experience, and skills a well as their culture, preferences, and biases. It also helps you to evaluate their present capability and future potential.

Next, casual conversations among members of your team can serve as the glue that binds people together and builds strength in team or company relationships. Encouraging the development of relationships, through casual conversation among people who work together every day, helps build a sense of common purpose.

In my experience, people who know each other on a more personal level are more likely to support each other when it comes to getting the work done, especially when the going gets tough. Their ability to communicate with each other beyond casual conversation also gets that much easier.

Leaders who engage in everyday conversations with those they lead invariably reveal something of themselves. It takes them from the realm of "boss" to the more approachable place of "boss who is also human."

If you want those under your charge to participate with you in achieving your collective goals and to make contributions that go beyond simply doing what they're told, you must put something of yourself in the mix. People will only share information about themselves if you show you're willing to meet them halfway and share something of yourself, too.

If you use casual conversation as a way of building strong relationships among your team, between you and your peers, and also to some extent with those to whom you report, it has a way of facilitating the flow of useful information throughout the organization.

There is however, an important caveat.

Casual conversations can go from being constructive and helpful to divisive and destructive if you fail to handle them with care. That's when they get in the way of building healthy, productive working environments. To avoid this, there are a few things to consider when engaging in casual conversation at work. Use these simple guidelines as a framework for maintaining both a congenial and productive work environment.

KEEP YOUR CONVERSATIONS FRIENDLY AND PROFESSIONAL. People don't need or want to know all of the intimate details of your life. Providing too much information (as in, whoa! too much information!) could be embarrassing and the very thing that will have people avoiding you rather than seeking you out. Seek balanced two-way conversations that give each participant the opportunity to take part.

KNOW WHEN A CONVERSATION IS OVER AND MOVE ON. Conversations that outlive their usefulness can, and do, get in the way of getting the work done. Spending inordinate amounts of time leaning on door frames or hanging over cubicle walls talking about whatever is not the idea at all. Keep your exchanges short yet friendly. Everyone will appreciate it.

RESIST, AT ALL COSTS, ANY TEMPTATION TO PARTICIPATE IN IDLE GOSSIP OR RUMOUR MONGERING. When rumour, innuendo, and other negative lines of conversation enter the environment, bad feelings and damaged relationships are quick to follow. As leader, you set the tone. As such, it is important to model constructive and helpful conversations and to be clear that you do not condone negative talk.

Office Politics

Ah, office politics. It's not a subject that people like to spend a lot of time discussing. However, office politics is a fact of organizational life. It can hold sway over the kind of working environment you create. And it can either support or get in the way of authentic communication.

Office politics is about power and advantage: how we acquire it and how we use it to influence others, sometimes for our own benefit, and sometimes for the benefit of a larger purpose.

I know what you're thinking. You think about office politics and immediately go to the dark side, conjuring up images of some very slick people engaging exclusively in self-indulgent activities to the detriment of the common interest. But politics in organizational life doesn't have to be self-serving or destructive. It can be a useful communication tool. So, in an attempt to distinguish the baby from the bath water here's my take on the bad, the ugly, and the good.

. . .

BAD OFFICE POLITICS AND SELF-PROMOTION

Self-promotion is not necessarily a bad thing. After all, when we accomplish something great, it is not wrong to feel pride or to talk about it. However, self-promotion crosses a line when it takes precedence over the achievement of shared goals. Someone who spends inordinate amounts of unproductive time tapping into the organizational grapevine (a repository for incomplete information and throwaway commentary) to determine who to suck up to next, or what tidbit of information might be useful as a questionable tool of "persuasion" is engaged in bad office politics.

Bad office politics is where gossip and innuendo lie. It represents the swampy edges of organizational life, and it is no wonder that most people have little tolerance for it.

UGLY OFFICE POLITICS AND DESTRUCTIVE BEHAVIOUR

Office politics gets ugly when someone takes self-promotion to greater depths. People who practice ugly office politics are not above taking credit for other people's work. They are crafty, good at placing blame on others for their own mistakes. Bullying is ugly office politics. These are all practices that can make organizational life intolerable.

GOOD OFFICE POLITICS = BUILDING POSITIVE RELATIONSHIPS

If bad and ugly office politics are the bath water, then this is where the baby comes in. It's where opportunity lies.

You, as a leader in the middle, must engage in relationship building to get things done. You have to go beyond the confines of your own area to build purposeful and focussed relationships with people in a variety of roles, levels, and situations. You do this:

- to understand and stay focussed on the purpose and larger objectives of the organization

- to forge mutually beneficial alliances with others both inside and outside the organization
- to make certain you get the resources you need to accomplish your goals
- to keep lines of communication open

Building relationships means spending time with people at all levels of the organization, finding out what makes them tick, giving support to their goals, and using your power of persuasion to contribute to situations where everyone gets to win. This is the nature of good office politics.

The practice of good office politics relies on three things:

- good moral compass
- generous attitude toward others, and
- interest in forging collaborative relationships for the purpose of gaining collective strength, learning, and growth

There's a bonus that comes with the practice of good office politics: the respect and goodwill you'll earn from the people you work with. I have observed that people who practice good office politics often have all the recognition and accolades they can handle.

And that can't be bad.

Straight Talk

The practice of good office politics involves engaging in straight talk. There's a movie called *Straight Talk.* It's about a young woman who was accidentally hired by a radio station to give advice to the lovelorn. This young woman was delightfully guileless, dishing out her unadorned advice with clarity and good humour. Her counsel to one caller, who was obviously playing the martyrdom card, went something like, "Get down off the cross honey. Somebody needs the wood!" It made me smile. It also made me think about how important straight talk is in leading and ensuring clarity in communication practices.

ou practice straight talk, you increase your chance of cutting
ifusion and allowing for quicker problem solving. Straight talk
values truth, builds trust, and grows integrity. What's not to like about
that? And yet, people in so many organizations are incredibly bad at it.

Large, bureaucratic organizations have trouble with straight talk,
with their acronyms and jargon. Some people believe that the more
complicated or obscure the language, the more important the message.
And, of course, there are always the bad and ugly office politics
muddying the waters in the background.

As a leader in the middle you may have been on the receiving end of
missives full of superfluous language and directives that required
several readings before a glimmer of understanding dawned. It happens.

What can you do about it?

Aside from challenging up and asking for clarity, you may not have
control over gobbledygook that comes to you from on high. What you do
have control over is the clarity and veracity of the messages you dispatch
and the environment you create within your own sphere of operations.

This means establishing a clear set of principles for communicating
with others no matter where in the organization your messages go. Here
are some examples.

PRINCIPLE # 1: TALK TO THE ORGAN GRINDER, NOT THE MONKEY.

When we talk to the wrong person (or people) about something, we
often do it to gain support or sympathy for our position. It doesn't
usually solve anything and can create ill feeling and speculation that's
unnecessary.

PRINCIPLE #2: THIS ORGANIZATION IS A JARGON-FREE ZONE.

You may have gathered by now that I'm a fan of simple language.
Business jargon (or any kind of jargon for that matter) may sound more
intelligent or important, but it doesn't foster understanding and does
contribute to poor communication.

PRINCIPLE #3: SERVE WHILE FRESH.

Feedback goes stale. The longer we take to share information with each other, the less value it will have for us. Ask permission... then deliver it when it's fresh. For one thing, it'll be easier to remember and that alone makes it more useful.

PRINCIPLE #4: PEOPLE ARE NOT PUNISHED FOR SPEAKING THEIR MINDS.

Often people are reticent to speak up for fear of ridicule or some other subtle form of punishment. Taking the hammer out of the communication toolbox allows for more open and meaningful conversation.

PRINCIPLE #5: EVERYONE HAS SOMETHING IMPORTANT TO SAY.

Adherence to this principle makes a promise to those who may be reticent to speak up that their opinions count.

PRINCIPLE #6: LISTEN FIRST...TALK LATER.

Listening is part of having respectful and candid conversations. It allows for good questions. Good questions invite thoughtful answers, which in turn increase the quality of conversations.

PRINCIPLE #7: R-E-S-P-E-C-T IS BOTH A NOUN AND VERB.

This principle (otherwise known as the Aretha Franklin principle) pretty much speaks for itself. Without it, the chances of establishing a culture of straight talk are pretty dim.

Establishing Standards for Optimal Communication Practices

Along with the seven straight talk principles, you will want to establish some standards around your communication practices: transparency, sincerity, civility, and even curiosity. These values are a litmus test for the accuracy and intent of your messages.

Transparency...How Much Light Do You Let In?

In organizational life, transparency involves openness—in the information we share and the way we communicate with each other. In the larger context, transparency is important to the creation and maintenance of dynamic, resilient organizations because it invites everyone to fully participate and take responsibility (and credit) for decisions made and goals achieved.

In the context of leading from the middle, transparency asks you to be accessible as a leader and also to show your humanness. By doing so, you invite those you lead to do the same, potentially increasing everyone's level of transparency and facilitating more open communication between you.

The question of transparency usually lies not in what is being transmitted but how much? There are things that get in the way of wider disclosure. And they usually have to do with vulnerability.

Sometimes we keep things about ourselves hidden for fear of being judged. People often mistakenly equate vulnerability to weakness, when in reality it is quite the opposite.

Whatever the reason, choosing transparency means you choose to be accessible to those you lead (and those who lead you). As a result you will engender greater trust and increase the clarity of your communications with others.

How might you accomplish this?

The Johari Window

The Johari Window[1] is a model developed by Joseph Luft and Harrington Ingham to help people gain a better understanding of themselves, their communication practices, and the possibilities for sharing more openly with others.

The upper left pane of the window represents *my public self.* This is where thoughts and feelings have already been openly expressed. It's stuff about us that everybody knows. For instance, I have brown hair (most of the time).

The upper right pane represents my blind spots. These are the things others see in us that we don't. For example, a colleague once told me that he saw me as aloof. This took me by surprise because it wasn't how I saw myself at all. But, when I looked at the information more closely, I began to realize how he might have gained that impression. And that was useful.

The third pane of the window highlights *my hidden self.* This is knowledge that we have about ourselves that we choose not to share with others. For instance I... Oh, never mind.

The final pane is the area reserved for *my unconscious self.* This is the stuff we don't know that we don't know.

To create greater transparency using the Johari Window, the goal is to increase the size of the public self by:

- exposing more blind spots
- showing more of ourselves to others, thus reducing the area of our hidden self

That's the theory. Here's a simple story to illustrate how it might work.

I once played a round of golf with a woman I didn't know very well. Her name was Betty. On meeting, Betty and I were polite to each other, exchanging the usual pleasantries, but we didn't share the camaraderie that makes playing pleasant.

As we worked our way through the course, Betty and I talked. I learned more about her life and she learned more about mine. As a consequence, our picture of each other grew with each new revelation. We compared opinions, attitudes, and experiences. And, as we walked off the eighteenth green, we were laughing about many of life's ironies. The game itself was of little consequence. Neither of us scored very well (which gave us something else in common) but we walked off the course with much more than we had when we first began, which was a better understanding of one another, increased level of respect and friendship.

To apply the Johari Window to this scenario, when Betty and I started our game, the area of our public self was very small, and the blind spots and secrets areas quite large. However, by the end of the game, public self had increased as we shared information about ourselves with each other. Our blind spots reduced to accommodate the shift in our own particular views.

It's largely the same in the workplace. To increase the area of your public self, you could, for instance:

- solicit feedback from others in an effort to bring your blind spots into the light
- test the waters of vulnerability by daring to share more of yourself, perhaps enough to encourage others to do the same

I know. It's not easy. However, in the context of opening up lines of communication and getting the most out of your interactions with others, the level of transparency you achieve will affect the quality of the information you both give and receive and the pace at which you achieve mutual understanding.

· · ·

SINCERITY

Sincerity may not be the first word that comes to mind when you think about successful leadership. It's one of those "soft" words that is sometimes overlooked in the frenetic activities of the day. And yet, one of the foundations of effective communication is believing in your message enough to want others to understand it and to accept it as a true representation of you and your view. That's sincerity. It's about representing yourself genuinely without guile or hypocrisy.

Okay, maybe it's not that simple... not in the real world anyway. There are a lot of temptations out there, temptations to pretend we are more knowledgeable, more experienced, more skilled, more empathetic, more important, even wealthier than we really are. The thing is, good leadership is rarely about any of that and, as already mentioned, is rarely about you.

As a leader in the middle, you may have the opportunity to choose other people for leadership roles in your organization. If not, you will no doubt have input into choosing people who work under your supervision. So, you must not only be personally vigilant about your own sincerity but also be on the lookout for it on the occasions when you are choosing people to work with you.

It's not easy to spot, I grant you. It will require you to look beyond words for consistency and alignment of words and actions. And it will require you to acknowledge your own foibles. I have yet to meet any paragons of virtue among my friends, relatives, or acquaintances. The closest I ever came to it was the day, a very long time ago, after I had ratted out my sister for doing something naughty, that she accused me of being a *virgin of paragon* which of course is an entirely different thing.

On a more serious note, I'm reminded of a time when I attended a function where sincerity, my own included, was notably absent.

It was Christmas time and our organization participated in a number of activities to support charitable causes. Often, we would buy a table at a luncheon benefit with net proceeds going to the charity in question.

On this one particular winter's day, eight of us were walking from the office building to such a luncheon being hosted at an upscale hotel a few blocks away.

We walked in a bunch, all well wrapped and well shod, happily chatting together about nothing terribly important. There were other bunches of business people as well, equally well-dressed, walking in the same direction.

About a block from our destination, we passed a man sitting on the sidewalk. His hair and beard were long and stringy and he held in his hand a Styrofoam cup and a sign that said something like, *Hungry. Please help.*

I suppose none of us will really know whether or not this man was representing himself sincerely, but he was obviously not doing very well.

My group and I, engrossed in our conversation and barely noticing the man, walked past him.

The people walking behind us did the same, with one exception. One man stopped long enough to look at the man and say, "Get a job."

On hearing this, I remember feeling ashamed of myself for not acknowledging the man or giving him something to ease the pain of his day. I also remember feeling appalled and outraged by the other man's "get a job" comment. It was an ignorant, throwaway remark that lacked compassion and decency.

But we all moved on, in a hurry, not to be late for our important luncheon.

We reached our table and seated ourselves. A few minutes later Mr. Get-a-Job and his colleagues also entered the room. The irony of this story became clear then. We were all there in support of the Salvation Army to help raise funds for the vital work they do to ease the lives of people just like the man we had seen sitting on the sidewalk... and so conveniently ignored.

On that day, it was clear that although we were physically present at the luncheon, we had left our sincerity behind, choosing instead to focus on being seen to do the right thing rather than actually doing it.

Sadly, I don't think this story is particularly unique. There are times when all of us lose sight of our sincerity for the sake of something deemed more important. But know that in your interactions with others, sincerity matters. It builds trust and will help you build an environment where transparency in your dealings with others becomes easier.

. . .

CIVILITY

Some may believe that civility is a minor consideration at work, especially when you are constantly plagued by looming deadlines and demands. Who has time to be polite? Who has time to say "please" and "thank you" or stop to consider the effect your behaviour is having on those around you? And why should you care as long as you're getting the job done?

Well, I think you have to care and you have to make time. Here are at least four reasons why:

1. Successful collaboration isn't possible without it. Collaboration is a key in today's workplace. When you work together with others to achieve a common, mutually beneficial goal, it is often the case that impatience and disagreement will raise its ugly head and start goading you into saying things you might not otherwise entertain. It is at these times when a good dose of civility is required. Rude and self-indulgent remarks simply get in the way of achieving a satisfactory outcome.

2. How people treat each other inside the organization will reverberate, for good or ill, outside the organization. Those who work in an atmosphere where good manners are the norm will respond to their customers and others in kind. There's nothing complicated about that. And for some reason, it's my guess that customers are more willing to part with their money if they feel they're being treated with respect.

3. People make their best effort when they feel acknowledged and important. I started my work life in the mailroom of a bank. My job was to open mail and deliver it to its intended recipients in a department of approximately three hundred people. Many department managers either completely ignored me or made me the unfortunate recipient of rude and bad-tempered remarks. A few, however, received their mail with good grace, responding with a well-placed thank you and a smile. When this happened, I felt I was doing something of value. It was a small

gesture but always with a big result and a willingness on my part to do more for those managers who had taken the time to acknowledge my existence, despite my lowly placement on the hierarchical ladder.

4. Civility is key to building relationships and reputations through social media. Today, workplaces extend beyond walls and borders through technology. No doubt you send emails, text messages, and tweets every day to bosses, colleagues and employees, some of whom you may never have met face-to-face. To me, civility is an important part of communicating through these and other media. After all, when you say something on social media, no matter the vehicle, it is captured forever and you can't take it back. And it shapes the image you create of yourself which can either reflect who you really are or cast a shadow that is difficult to overcome. As a leader in the middle, this is true not only of you but of the department, region or division you represent.

Some people might take pride in their ability to rattle others with rude behaviour. They say things like, "This is who I am. Get used to it."

But civility is not about who we are. It is about how we choose to behave. And insisting on good manners simply makes sense.

Curiosity

While civility is a significant part of good communication and indeed good leadership, we can become so careful about not offending that our communication becomes overly vague, and curiosity is stifled. Of course it is important to be sensitive to others and respectful of how they like to be viewed and addressed. However, don't let political correctness get in the way of a curious mind because curiosity is the fuel of progress.

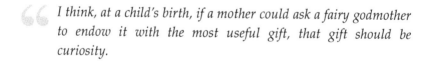

I think, at a child's birth, if a mother could ask a fairy godmother to endow it with the most useful gift, that gift should be curiosity.

ELEANOR ROOSEVELT

I think fairy godmothers everywhere are quite liberal with the gift of curiosity when we are born. Somehow though, along the way, so many of us wrap the gift up again and put it away in our inner attics, unwrapping it only on occasion. I think we do that because, as we grow, we are taught that curiosity can be intrusive, impolite, and get us into trouble. But I think it is one of the foundations of good leadership.

As a fundamental tool for exploration, curiosity is the springboard to developing our ability to ask good questions. And the skill of asking questions is one that all good leaders must have in their tool kit. To me, a good question is one that evokes deep thought, instigates change, inspires creativity in others, and/or clears the debris of confusion to make room for clarity. It can come from no other place than our very human tendency to want to know. And, for many of us, it requires blowing off the cobwebs of our childhood gift and putting it to use.

So, if you haven't invited your curiosity out to play lately, what might be getting in the way?

1. You confuse curiosity with being nosy.

Many of us, as we grow, are schooled to mind our own business. It is offensive to pry or stare. It's annoying when we ask too many questions. And later, as adults, it is easy to see why we hesitate to ask when we want to know something.

There's a difference between being curious and being nosy. It centres on intent. Those who seek information with the intent to use what they come to know for the purpose of passing judgment and gaining leverage over others are more likely to be considered nosy. Or worse.

Alternately, those who seek information out of genuine interest do so with the intent to explore, discover, and expand their knowledge. These people have a way of engaging others in the exploration and making them feel valued rather than scrutinized.

In other words, curiosity comes from a place of innocence and fascination.

2. You believe you need to have all the answers before you ask the questions.

Some leaders fear that asking a question could make them look naive or ignorant, tarnishing their image, or bringing their capability as a leader into question. And so, they simply stop asking, and instead live in hope that someone else will ask the *dumb* question. In this we run risk of restricting the amount of useful information and ideas available to us. And, we rarely learn how to ask those really good questions. No one has all the answers.

The trouble is that focusing on our own image does not get the job done. And, it does not allow for the kind of exploration required to build and grow the organization to its full potential.

Your image is built by how you behave, the quality of your relation-ships, and the results you achieve. Others will soon see that your "dumb" questions get you and your team rather a lot farther than those who cower in fear over what other people might or might not think.

3. You haven't made curiosity part of your working style.

Simply put, if you do not make inquiry, exploration, and discovery part of the fabric of your working day, you will inhibit your collective curiosity muscles. Leaders who want to create and encourage this kind of environment must do so by going first, showing others how it's done, and acknowledging those who follow their example. As a leader in the middle, this means being purposefully interested in what is going on in the environment above, below, and all around you. This is a way to stay connected and up-to-date. And it is a way to ensure the communication you have with others carries meaning that they can understand with minimal brow furrowing.

So, yes, communicating with others is not as simple as it looks. And yet, I'm thinking, if you work on creating the right conditions and constantly strive for truth and clarity without gumming it up with jargon and rhetoric, you'd accomplish so much more.

THINK ABOUT IT

Q. What do you pride yourself in when it comes to sending new information out to your team? How might you build on your communication successes?

Q. What is your biggest communication obstacle? What might be happening that is causing this? What has to be different to make things better? What role do you play in bringing it about?

Q. As a middle leader, how do you encourage the good kind of office politics and discourage the ugly and the bad kinds? What could you do more of? Less of?

Q. What does your Johari window look like? If your windowpane of public knowledge were larger, how would it serve you and those you lead? What would you have to do to make that happen?

NOTES

6

RECEPTION

 To listen well is as powerful a means of communication and influence as to talk well.

JOHN MARSHALL

How you choose to react to the data you receive makes the difference between success and failure, both in the relationships you develop and the decisions you make about life and work.

In this chapter we'll address the challenge of determining what's useful and accurate in the barrage of messages coming at you. We'll talk about how you make those judgements and how to craft the most effective response by:

- listening deeply to imprint what is being said long enough to recall it when needed
- examining received information with a critical eye to discern accuracy and truth (critical thinking)
- staying in control of your natural tendency to jump to conclusions
- sharing incoming information with those under your charge

> with a view to achieving common understanding from the
> original source to the end receiver

There is an increasing amount of false information circulating online and in the workplace. Some of it is harmless fun. Some of it has a darker, more sinister side whose purpose is to manipulate you into believing something that, while untrue, will serve a certain special interest. Information can easily get snagged, bruised, and punctured on grapevines, full of the bitter fruit of gossip, where it becomes distorted and unreliable. When knowledge is power, you've no doubt encountered people who will cling to it for the sake of maintaining leverage over others.

Whatever the reason, if incoming information is to be at all helpful and enlightening, you must learn how to subject it to rigorous scrutiny.

Listening and Remembering

I often wonder how much information we can actually recall simply from listening to someone talk. Taking notes is one way of ingesting new information, but sometimes it just isn't convenient or appropriate. Often, we have to rely on what we can remember.

If you're like me, that's a scary thought. My memory for some things is pretty awful. I'm working on it, and a little research tells me my memory doesn't have to be awful if I give regular exercise to my memory muscle. The same holds true for you.

There is a certain magic in remembering small things that may not seem important to you but are immensely satisfying to others. These small details, like remembering someone's name, can have a big impact on how that person responds to you. In fact, simple acts of acknowledgement are very powerful.

Many years ago, when I was working as a personnel officer in the head office of the bank, I was invited to attend a breakfast and listen to the president and chairman of the board talk about our goals and challenges.

Before we sat down to breakfast, the chairman, a stocky fair-haired man in his fifties, took a turn about the room, which held about 350 people, a fraction of the 35,000 employees of the bank worldwide. He

happened upon me quite by accident. I introduce(
for a very brief time. Then he moved on.

After the eggs and while servers poured mo:
got up to speak. He wasn't tall or physica
commanded attention. He eloquently described t
and painted a realistic picture of the challe
employees of the bank.

And then the magic happened. He said something like, "I was talking to Gwyn earlier and she reminded me of the importance of people to our organization."

Until that moment I had felt a small, insignificant part of the bank's lofty and global goals. That all changed with one simple word and the phrase in which it was included. I was no longer a blurred face in the crowd or a very small cog in a very large wheel. I felt what I had to say had mattered and I had been heard. I developed a new respect for the chairman and no longer saw him as an untouchable, unknowable figure-head ensconced in his top-floor, glass-walled corner office. He was real because he showed me I was real to him. I paid more attention after that to everything he said and did.

You may not be a CEO, but your ability to engage those under your charge, your peers, and even your bosses will be greatly enhanced by listening for and remembering the small details of your conversations with them. Granted, it's a discipline. And it's not easy to master. But it also works wonders.

The Power of Critical Thinking

Clarity is one of your greatest tools as both an individual and a leader, regardless of where you sit on the organization chart. To achieve it, you have to be able to mentally process the plethora of available information and determine its value before drawing conclusions and acting on them. This is where critical thinking is essential to making sound decisions with confidence.

One of the things that gets in the way of our ability to think critically is the way we process incoming information, particularly as it pertains to ᴇr fuzzy distinctions we tend to make between facts, inferences, ᴏns, and assumptions.

The critical thinker's goal in processing new information is to get as close to fact as possible. Facts are hard evidence. The further away we get from fact, the less reliable our evidence will be. Clearly identifying sources of information and putting them in the proper perspective is an important leadership skill. This does not mean to suggest that facts are the only basis on which you will make a decision. However, it does allow you to place value on the information you receive and guide your decision-making process accordingly.

Here's a simple example of what I mean when we draw conclusions based on our personal observations. I developed this schematic in collaboration with my colleague Maureen Hannah to illustrate the possible conclusions that could be drawn from available information about students in a classroom.

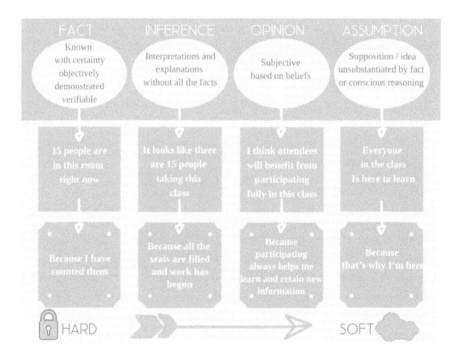

FACT: something known with certainty that can be objectively demonstrated and verified.

INFERENCE: an interpretation of events that provides explanations for situations in which all of the facts are not available or yet to be determined.

OPINION: an objective statement based on personal beliefs.

ASSUMPTION: a supposition or idea that is unsubstantiated by fact or conscious reasoning.

In any gathering of people, know that facts, inferences, opinions, and assumptions will be present. The next time you go into a meeting, take a moment to think about how you'll recognize, use, or challenge them in service of reaching accurate conclusions. By doing so, your chances of also making good decisions will be that much better.

While you won't want to examine everything you see and hear in a microscopic way, it's important to understand that often, the conclusions we draw can differ from the conclusions others draw about the same thing—depending on whether the thinking stopped at assumption or made an effort to get closer to fact.

Ladder of Inference

The Ladder of Inference, a concept developed by Chris Argyris, is designed to help us understand and explain how we arrive at our conclusions and to check out where we might need to conduct further exploration.

Once we get to the top of the ladder of inference, we act on our conclusions.

One rung down, we draw conclusions that reinforce our views.

We add our own meaning based on assumptions we make, inferences we see, and opinions and biases we hold.

The data we select is influenced by previous experiences, views, and beliefs.

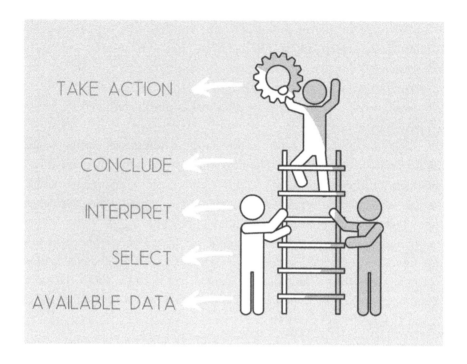

I think it safe to say that most human beings spend quite a bit of time going up the ladder only to find that their conclusions are based on the wrong information.

Here's an example of what I mean.

One day, while at the supermarket, I was waiting at the checkout counter behind a mother and her little boy, who looked to be about three years old. Together they had two carry baskets brimming with grocery items.

Realizing she had forgotten something, Mom left the queue to go and get it, suggesting to her son that he begin to put the items they had already collected onto the counter. He was very small. In fact, so small his ability to comply with this suggestion was in some doubt, at least in my mind. But soon he was grabbing each item and chucking it as high as he could over his head so that it landed, rather unceremoniously, on the counter above him.

He was doing fine until he came to a can of soup. After heaving this in the direction of the other items, it landed on its side. Being fearful it might roll off the counter and hit him on the head, I took the can and set it right, thinking I was doing him a service.

The little boy gave me a filthy look. He looked at the can. Then he looked at me and scowled. And, when his mother returned from her quest, he said, "Something's not right."

Mom, not really understanding what her son was saying, asked him what was not right, at which point, I said, "I think he's referring to me. I righted the can of soup so it wouldn't roll off the counter. I was trying to help."

To this, the little boy raised himself up to his full height of maybe three feet and loudly proclaimed, "I didn't want any help!"

While a little stunned by the vehemence of his words, I quickly apologized to him, received some words of thanks from Mom, and then decided it might be best if I minded my own business.

If we were to apply this story to the Ladder of Inference, it would look something like this:

At the bottom of the ladder is information that is clear and observable, in other words, *fact*. In this case, I saw a little boy helping his mother with the grocery shopping. I saw, too, there were a lot of groceries and the little boy was really small.

I climbed to the second rung from the bottom where I narrowed my focus and selected only the data that interested me. In this case, I concentrated on two things, the little boy and his attempts to hurl grocery items onto the counter above him.

I climbed to the third rung of the ladder and began to make assumptions. First, I assumed that because he was small, he was not really capable of fulfilling his assigned task. And then, I assumed he needed help.

I climbed to the fourth rung of the ladder and concluded, based on these assumptions, that he would be glad of my help. From there, I proceeded to the fifth rung where I connected this conclusion to my belief that helping each other is an important and natural part of the human experience.

When I got all the way to the top of the ladder and acted in accordance with my assumptions and beliefs, I was met with hostility rather than the appreciation, or at least neutrality, I was expecting.

It is easy for us to run up the ladder and get things wrong even when we have the best of intentions. Had I simply asked the little boy if he would like help in unloading his groceries (or in his case up-loading his groceries), I would have had the answer I needed, respected his wishes, and stayed out of trouble. But I didn't. So I didn't.

Good leadership can falter quite easily if we fail to check out and validate information we receive or assumptions we make about it before we form an opinion and take action.

In today's environment, where taking liberties with the truth has become commonplace, taking the time to check sources and validate conclusions also means saving the time it takes to correct an action based on wrong assumptions or incomplete information.

The Importance of Observation

On a similar note, we're big on jumping into action, at least in western society. Sometimes doing so leads us to big things. At other times, our only reward for leaping into busy work before spending any time at all finding out what's actually going on is chaos.

Many moons ago I was part of a team-building course in Toronto. At one point, the facilitator divided us into groups and marched us outside to tackle a project that involved climbing poles and traversing from one pole to the other with only the aid of ropes and some safety tackle. Our goal was to successfully overcome the obstacles put in our way and complete the course in the best possible time.

My group failed miserably. Not only did we not complete the course, we failed to overcome most of the obstacles as well.

With booby prize shamefully in hand, we reviewed what we might have done differently. And, in thinking about it now, apart from doing just about everything wrong, we simply didn't spend enough time in "O."

"O" stands for observation. It is part of a mental process that Edgar Schein, in his book *Process Consultation: Lessons for Managers and Consultants*, refers to as O.R.J.I.

Here's how it works.

Typically, when faced with a predicament, the human psyche follows a pattern.

We *observe* and get a picture of what is going on.

We *react* emotionally to our understanding of what's happening.

We *judge,* and draw conclusions based on our understanding and how it makes us feel.

We *intervene,* making decisions and taking action based on what we see, feel, and conclude.

In the case of my deplorable "team" experience, we spent a nanosecond really looking at the challenge before us or trying to understand it. We asked no questions of either the coordinators or each other. We did not inspect the obstacle course or make any kind of effort to evaluate the resources available to us, human or otherwise. The loudest voice took the lead. The action-oriented ones chomped at the bit to get out in the field and do something. And, the reflectors, being completely overwhelmed by the noise and confusion, registered what can only be described as insipid protests about making a plan first, an offering that, not surprisingly, fell on deaf ears.

Staying in *observation* is hard. When problems are pressing, emotions can work in opposition to rational thought, often wanting to take over at the most inadvisable and inconvenient times.

So, here are some ways to stay in *observation* and delay a move to action long enough to establish that the information you are working from is accurate.

Gather facts about the nature and scope of the problem. This means suspending, at least initially, feelings about what's going on long enough to get some solid data.

Take time to determine the resources and skills available to you. In the case of our team exercise, we spent no time at all determining *who knew what* or *who could do what.* As a result, a number of individual egos launched themselves into the project without knowing anything about the skills they had at their disposal or how they could best be used.

· · ·

Determine what you might be assuming about the situation and the people involved in it. Giving some time to validating assumptions is never a waste. Assumptions almost always hinder the process of getting at the true nature of a problem.

Make room for many questions and a variety of voices. This is simply about listening to every voice, be it soft or loud. And sometimes it is the dissenting voice that holds the clue to a solution.

The bottom line here is that great decisions rely on giving time to observation and critical thinking. Launching into action without thought might look good initially but will most certainly require more backtracking and remedial work than you likely have time for. As well, taking time to observe and think about what you do next is an action in itself. We human beings don't like to appear idle and so we come to believe that staying quietly in one place thinking and looking are tantamount to doing nothing. Just so you know, you aren't doing *nothing* if the outcome of your thinking and observation leads to your making effective decisions more often and leading to actions that consistently achieve great results.

Pass It On

As a leader in the middle, you will no doubt receive information that you're required to share with those under your charge. This passing along of information can have its own challenges. It's sort of like a party game. Someone whispers something in your ear. You pass it on to the next person. They pass it on to the next person after that and so it goes until the very last person has to tell everyone at the party what they heard. You know how it goes. The end message usually bears no resemblance at all to the original. Everybody laughs.

While the party game is usually fun, there is no room for this kind of "pass it on" communication style in the workplace. And yet it happens to everyone at some time or another. To minimize its effect and avoid people acting on inaccurate data or without commitment, your role, (after understanding the meaning and intent of the message yourself), is to ensure that in passing it along, you have the best opportunity to achieve a common understanding about what is being asked.

Part of this is deciding if you agree or not because passing on information when you agree is infinitely easier than doing so when you don't.

Indeed, when you don't agree you are faced with a couple of choices: align with your team, or align with the organization.

ALIGN WITH YOUR TEAM

When you're tasked with passing on information you don't agree with, this response option is easy in the short term but could create problems for you down the line. When you choose to align with your team and cast aspersions on the instruction from on high, you might think you're protecting yourself by stating that you are delivering the message under duress.

It goes something like this:

"I just received this memo today. We're being asked to move from these premises to make room for a new department. I don't agree with it. It's very inconvenient, but we don't have a choice. So please don't shoot the messenger."

While this sort of communication tactic may temporarily take the heat off you, it does nothing to mitigate general disgruntlement about the inevitability of having to move. (Believe me, there will be disgruntlement if you as leader openly voice your disapproval.) Nor will it help you build strong relationships with your bosses and peers. In short, this response lacks leadership and also inhibits your opportunity to push out the boundaries of your influence in service of a more satisfactory outcome.

So the question is, what do you do instead?

ALIGN WITH THE ORGANIZATION

When you receive a communication that you either don't understand, don't agree with, or have different ideas about, first go to the source. This might mean giving voice to something that may go against popular opinion, or the views of those more senior to you. It also means you must be prepared to ask bold questions or offer an alternate solution and make a case for it to be considered. There are risks to this. Of course there are. However, there are times in your experience as a middle leader when you must stand up and say your piece before you can be heard. You may not always win, but you owe it to yourself and those who follow you to try.

There is something very satisfying about challenging a policy or directive and having your ideas about it taken under advisement, especially when in the end you manage to affect change for the better. As you know, it won't happen every time. Sometimes you have to be satisfied with compromise. Sometimes too, the best you can get is a deeper understanding of why things are the way they are. Then you can do your best to support that.

That brings us back to the matter of sharing communication with your team when you have concerns about it.

Having made your inquiries and your case, (even if you didn't get your way and still don't agree), your job becomes one of support for your team and the greater organization. That means you do your best to present the facts as you know them. Allow time for opinion and questions from your team. Respond to these with as much objectivity as you can muster. Solicit their help. Then collectively focus on how you are going to get it done (whatever *it* happens to be) in as positive a manner as you can. In so doing, you will live to fight another day while keeping the lines of communication open without rancour from either your boss or your team.

As a final note, it's a different conversation altogether if you find yourself always disagreeing with the directives you receive from "on high." In this case, it is less about communication and more about compatibility with and alignment of philosophies and values. In such a case your decision becomes about you, what you want, and the personal choices you must face about how you are going to achieve it.

Arrogance

Arrogance is the great time waster. If you've failed at your attempts to engage in critical thinking, and you let assumptions rule your day, you will soon wade into the deep muck of arrogance.

We are all guilty of taking positions of arrogance. It doesn't discriminate. When it shows up, it has a way of impeding real progress, of serving the few at the expense of the many, and of making fools of those who put their own importance ahead of everything else.

Witness this exchange, which is an actual radio conversation between a US naval ship and Canadian authorities off the coast of Newfoundland. It was released by the Chief of US Naval Operations on October 10, 1995:

Americans: *Please divert your course fifteen degrees to the North to avoid a collision.*

Canadians: *Recommend you divert YOUR course fifteen degrees to the South to avoid a collision.*

Americans: *This is the Captain of a US Navy ship. I say again, divert YOUR course.*

Canadians: *No. I say again. You divert YOUR course.*

Americans: *THIS IS THE AIRCRAFT CARRIER USS LINCOLN, THE SECOND LARGEST SHIP IN THE UNITED STATES' ATLANTIC FLEET. WE ARE ACCOMPANIED BY THREE DESTROYERS, THREE CRUISERS AND NUMEROUS SUPPORT VESSELS. I DEMAND THAT YOU CHANGE YOUR COURSE FIFTEEN DEGREES NORTH, THAT'S ONE FIVE DEGREES NORTH, OR COUNTER MEASURES WILL BE UNDERTAKEN TO ENSURE THE SAFETY OF THIS SHIP.*

Canadians: *This is a lighthouse. It's your call.*

I saw two kinds of arrogance in this story. The first was the more obvious, being the attitude of the American naval captain. The second was the subtler but equally culpable Canadian authority who, rather than point out the Americans' mistake early in the exchange, actually strung them along knowing that eventually they would be shown as the foolish ones. It was a battle of egos and, while amusing for onlookers, totally unnecessary.

In the End

In communication, whether you are sending messages or receiving them, I've learned one big thing. It is that no matter how eloquent you are or how much you focus on achieving clarity, in the end, it will be your attitude that decides how effective you are in getting your message across in the way you mean it or comprehending an incoming message in the way it was meant.

THINK ABOUT IT

Q. If you could improve one thing about your ability to listen, what would it be? Why is that thing important? What would you start doing or stop doing that would help you get better at it?

Q. When you receive new information, how often do you make distinctions between fact and the other softer stuff: inference, opinion, and assumption? What value do you think making those distinctions would bring to your ability to gain clarity from the messages you receive and subsequently have to share?

Q. Think of a time when you "ran up" the Ladder of Inference. How did it work out for you? What might you do to minimize false assumptions and slow down your climb up the Ladder of Inference?

NOTES

SECTION III: WORKING TOGETHER

7

WORKING TOGETHER

Companies are communities. There's a spirit of working together. *Communities are not a place where a few people allow themselves to be singled out as solely responsible for success.*

HENRY MINTZBERG

In many ways, your life as a middle leader is more complicated than it might once have been. Yet, no matter how sophisticated your systems and structures are, there is one fundamental truth. You are still dealing with human beings. This is the human nature side of business. And people in organizations, modern or traditional, must find ways to work together effectively because, as Henry Mintzberg so succinctly points out, companies are communities. They must accomplish things together no matter the complexity of their respective operations.

How they do it varies according to the prevailing conditions and situations. I think it safe to say that what is especially needed in the middle leader's toolbox are skills associated with mentoring, coaching, collaborating, problem solving, influencing, serving, and team building because in the end, people have to do the work and developing these skills allows for the work to get done well.

Mentoring and Coaching

Some people use the terms *mentor* and *coach* interchangeably. However, while similar, in practice they fulfil different purposes.

Mentorships are broad. They tend to focus on general career and personal development. Unless part of a formal program, mentorships begin and end casually with no particular timelines to define them. Mentors are often viewed as "go to" people, where others can go to noodle thoughts and ideas and to get a more experienced perspective.

Coaching is more task-specific. There are timelines associated with it and specific goals established between coach and protégé. The focus for coaching is on maximizing potential. Often, it takes someone else to see something in us that we don't see in ourselves. So, potential lurks within every person under your charge, perhaps yet to be exposed. As coach, it's your job to help him or her see it and then do something about it for the good of all.

Being a Mentor

At some point in your career, you may have either had a mentor or been a mentor. We don't always recognize, in any kind of official way, when mentorship becomes part of our lives. Often it just happens.

The traditional view of mentors and mentees is that older people with years of experience form amicable relationships with younger people with similar interests and ambitions. Then, drawing on their greater knowledge, the older ones provide advice and counsel to the younger ones about things that will help them move their lives forward.

While it's true that veterans can teach us lessons of the past, are they always the best people to show us the path to the future? Maybe. Maybe not.

For instance, no matter where you are on the technology learning curve, the one thing you'll know for sure is that to learn it, you have to consult those who have the experience. It's not certain you'll find a technology mentor among the older workers. It's possible, but not certain. So in this case, the traditional perspective on mentorship gets turned on its head.

In the end it matters less about whether mentors are older, younger, or the same age as the mentee. What matters is the learning and growth that comes from having a relationship with a mentor, learning that might not have been possible otherwise.

My own experience with mentors didn't involve a long-term "master and grasshopper" type of relationship. However, there have been mentoring moments. These have been times when someone in my life has taught me something through example, or opened a door that I could not have opened by myself. These people were as much mentors as the venerable teachers who play long-term roles in shaping the lives of their mentees. They just didn't stay in my life long enough for me to really know them. My gratitude to them, however, will last as long as I do because they gave without expectation of a return other than the satisfaction of knowing they helped another struggling human being.

Mary: More Than a Boss

Mary was my first boss in human resources. She was looking for an assistant and having rifled through the roster of internal candidates that might fit her bill, she found me in the internal audit department correcting errors that our fledgling computer system had thrown up the previous day. She may also have found me yawning.

Initially, I was very flattered to be the chosen one until I learned Mary's selection criteria. Let's just say it was less than scientific. Specifically, she gave me the job because I could type; I cleaned up reasonably well; and I hadn't ticked anyone off...yet. Nonetheless, it was a step up for me into an area of work where I felt an affinity, so despite the dubious selection standards, I was happy to be there.

Mary was more than a boss to me. She taught me things about surviving in a male-dominated, traditional organization that went beyond how to fit in. She showed me the importance of knowing when to compromise and when to argue for something better or different.

Like the rest of us, Mary was not perfect. Her personal life was often in turmoil. Things got on her nerves that would slide off the backs of other people, like water off a duck. And, true to the legend of many red-headed people, Mary had a wicked temper. While always kind and generous toward me, with her colleagues she tended to be less disciplined. I know this because I once overheard her tell one of her male counterparts, "Oh, go pee in your hat and pull it down over your ears!"

Mary was my sounding board, a place to go where empathy lived and judgement didn't. Through her example, I learned that always looking my best was not just a thing that was nice to do. I learned to stand up for myself. I learned the importance of controlling my emotions and the negative impact on me, and others, when I don't.

Judy: Addressing Fear

I met Judy not long after arriving in Vancouver from Toronto. She was working for what was euphemistically referred to as an outplacement firm and as the bank, in its efforts to streamline operations, was doing quite a bit of out-placing, my path and Judy's crossed from time to time.

Judy had a graduate degree in counselling psychology. At the time of our meeting, I had no higher education to boast about and so I found Judy's academic credentials very impressive. She was also a kind person whose gentle demeanour suggested she was one who could be trusted. I liked that. It also suggested she had chosen the perfect profession for herself, and I wanted to know more about that.

Judy found something of a kinship in me for reasons I didn't know, but I wasn't going to question it. It was enough for me to have found a friend in a city where I was a stranger.

Through Judy, I learned that fearing doing something is not a good enough reason for not doing it. I learned this when we took a road trip together from San Francisco to Tucson, Arizona where we made a joint presentation to a group of Adlerian psychologists on the subject of outplacement counselling. Prior to this presentation, I was terrified to the point where I really thought I would not be able to do it.

It was at this point that Judy lost her patience with me. I might have done the same had I been in her shoes but her impatience was a wake-up call. I didn't want to let her down, and so I practiced in front of the mirror at every opportunity. And then I took my nervous, sweaty, nauseous self to the conference, stood up in front of a bunch of strangers, and began to talk.

I wasn't great. I knew it. Judy knew it. Yet, she was gracious and encouraging nonetheless. In spite of the outcome, the experience gave me a measure of confidence I hadn't known before because I had done something fearful... and survived.

Bill: Helping Me See My Own Abilities

Bill was a course instructor for City University where I first put my anxious toe into the waters of higher education. He was a brilliant teacher who had a way of inspiring and encouraging his students, most of whom were working to earn their MBAs. I felt like a fraud in a room full of people who really seemed to have their acts together. But Bill had a way of extracting our best thoughts and ideas and soon, I saw a glimmer of hope that what I thought might be fraudulent in me was actually a real ability to think critically and rationally. Who knew?

Bill played a huge role in helping me get into a graduate degree program. I did the work, but he opened the door.

Did he embody the typical image of a mentor? Not at all. Bill broke rules more often than most people, which landed him in a spot of bother now and again. And it's possible he was a little too fond of single malt Scotch. But I'm always going to remember him and be grateful for his being on my side when I most needed it.

These are some of my mentorship stories. You will have your own. Some of them might come from a formal mentoring arrangement, but mostly I think you'll discover that people who come into your life often go quietly out again but not without first opening a door for you to walk through and showing you something about yourself you might never have discovered on your own.

Three Requirements of Good Mentorship

What does it take to be a good mentor? Well, in my observation, there are three basic underpinnings to good mentorship.

1. INTEREST

The first requirement, interest, may seem obvious, but people undertake mentorships for different reasons. Not all of them are noble. For instance, there are some who may undertake it because they feel flattered at having been asked. Their egos have been stroked sufficiently for them to agree without considering the selflessness it takes to make such a relationship work well.

It is satisfying to think you have learned something well enough to be able to pass your knowledge on to another person. That's one of the rewards of being a mentor. However, those who are really not interested in another's career or life are not likely to take the time to understand what is needed in the relationship. That kind of arrangement tends to fizzle out before it really gets started.

Then there are the occasions when interest is missing from mentees. In this case, if a mentee is unwilling to consider, digest, or act on the guidance being offered, or fails to schedule meetings or take charge of the agenda, then the relationship is equally unbalanced.

So before considering your role as either mentor or mentee, ask yourself:

- What is it about this person that interests me?
- Why do I care?
- What do I see in this person that makes me want to spend time with him or her?

2. HONESTY

For a mentor/mentee relationship to reap reward, there must be honesty. Every such association should include a "no bullshit" clause. For instance, if you're a mentee but you are only hearing about how awesome you are, you're probably only getting half of the story. Half the story will not help you mitigate or eliminate the blind spots that get in the way of your personal progress. Conversely, if as mentor, you are holding back on sharing information with your mentee to be kind or perhaps avoid conflict, you are compromising the relationship and undermining what is most likely your sincere desire to help.

. . .

3. RESPECT

The third element in establishing good mentor/mentee relations is respect. For example, people of the older generation have their pride. They like the idea of mentoring someone younger because it seems to flow with the accepted order of things... you know, the master and grasshopper type of relationship. However, when it is the grasshopper doing the teaching, it can make a master feel somehow redundant, even stupid. And that's not something one willingly volunteers for.

Alternately, younger people may not see the benefits of slowing down to help the older ones learn things that to them are elementary. They may also feel they are carrying a load for someone who might even make more money than they do and from whom they see no reciprocal reward. That's not much fun either.

Being respectful of another person's situation means being patient. It means having the kindness to acknowledge that your mentee may not know what you know, but there are things they know that you don't. For mentorships to work ideally there should be enough respect and empathy to allow the mentor to appreciate the skills and knowledge of the mentee; and the mentee to give credence to the lessons that only the mentor can teach.

Some organizations have fairly sophisticated programs that allow compatible people to enter into a mentorship arrangement with each other. Mentors volunteer their time and prospective mentees choose from a roster of these willing and generous participants, usually based on what they want to learn and the respect they hold for the chosen mentor. There is a lot to be said for these programs. They provide a structured approach to sharing both practical knowledge and experiential wisdom. They also provide a certain amount of glue that ensures retention of an organization's best people. What's not to like about that?

It is possible to have people come into our lives that have something to teach us but are not, shall we say, ideal mentors or role models. In fact when I reflect on my own life, those who helped me steer through the rough spots were sometimes impatient, sometimes less than honest, sometimes not even particularly respectful. But they were never indifferent and always human.

In truth, we can learn from another person even if they express doubts about our abilities to rise to the occasion. That kind of relationship can call forth a defiant "I'll show you" mentality that takes us to a new level in spite of ourselves. Learning, and the growth that comes from it, can only be mortally wounded by complacency, indifference, or the expectation that it happens without effort.

There are opportunities everywhere for each of us to mentor and be mentored by other people. We don't have to wait to be invited to participate in a formal program. We don't have to be identified as rising stars in our organizations. We don't have to be perfect. We simply need to look to the people around us and think of them as potential teachers or potential students. If we do that, with a measure of interest, honesty and respect, it is possible for learning and the growth that comes from it, to happen.

Coaching

As a middle leader you might think your coaching opportunities are limited. Whether you are in charge of a large department or only a few people, you may be thinking the tools and time available to you for that sort of thing are not always readily at hand. Besides, the very idea of coaching sounds exhausting, doesn't it?

But wait. You already have to complete performance reviews on all of your direct reports. You're rolling your eyes to the ceiling right now, aren't you? I get it. The performance review seems to be universally dreaded and often for good reason. That's because although it starts out with noble intentions the process tends to degenerate into a meaningless, time-wasting exercise.

You might loathe the performance review because it's another thing to do. Employees tend to dislike them because they rarely acknowledge their real contribution while still being a determining factor in how much they are paid. The performance review often becomes something we do *to* people rather than *with* them. Like going to the dentist for root canal, we approach the task with a tinge of trepidation.

Some have even suggested that organizations do away with perfor-mance reviews altogether.

What a great idea. But wait...

Performance reviews could be an ideal coaching tool. Besides, if you take away the mechanism that helps you evaluate individual contribu-tion to the achievement of your group goals, how will you know what the individuals have done? How will you know what your people need to be successful? How will you know how to engage them? Or reward them? Or help them?

What I know is that this is not an annual *fill-out-a-form-without-much-thought-and-get-it-over-with* thing.

I think it's a leadership thing, a coaching thing, and a management thing.

Here's what you can do to transform the old notion of performance appraisals, as a general pain in the anatomical place of your choice, into a coaching opportunity that's useful and meaningful for you and each of your direct reports as participants in the process.

THE LEADERSHIP THING: LAYING THE GROUNDWORK

1. *Provide clarity about the big picture.* No one likes to work in a vacuum so it's important to make sure each person under your charge is clear about the vision, goals, and purpose of your team, department, or organization. In other words, clarity around the big picture provides people with a common view of what success will look like from one end of the year to the other.

2. *Provide resources for learning and growth where needed.* It's one thing to have a clear vision and set of goals. It's another to ensure that you have the capability to achieve them. It is a leadership responsibility to find out what is needed and to provide the tools that will allow the vision of success to become a reality. As a middle leader, you may have to lobby for the resources you need. That's where building relationships at all levels of your organization will come in handy.

3. *Remove obstacles.* The road to success is often littered with obstacles. Communication systems break down. Supplies dry up. Other unanticipated events get in the way. If you want people to fulfill your performance expectations, you must be prepared to pay attention to their journey by reducing the size of these obstacles to something they can reasonably negotiate.

THE COACHING THING: BEING SPONSOR AND CHAMPION

1. *Be clear about individual contribution to the vision of success.* This is about working with people individually to ensure they know what piece of the overall goal belongs to them and more specifically, the expectations you have in terms of what you want them to produce.
2. *Gain agreement.* This involves conversation. People will have questions, opinions, and even doubts about their assignment and your expectations. It's important to make time to listen and come to agreement about what will be needed, from both of you, to deliver a successful result.
3. *Encourage.* Sometimes the work gets hard or frustrating or discouraging. People need to know that you are in their corner as they go about meeting the expectations you and your organization have of them. A word of encouragement is often all it takes. That means having people on your radar all the time.
4. *Challenge.* When you have people regularly in the frame, you come to know what they are capable of. Sometimes, you will be able to see it more clearly than they can. Challenging them to go beyond what they believe they are capable of builds skill for the organization and confidence for the individual.
5. *Celebrate.* This is an often over-looked activity. However, acknowledging people for work well done, for accomplishments above and beyond expectations, or for life's other little victories, has a way of spurring us on and helping

us believe that we are engaged in something worthwhile. Do it often, with sincerity, and keep it simple. It doesn't have to be a big boo-rah to be appreciated.

THE MANAGEMENT THING: CONTROLLING THE PROCESS

1. *Make time.* As a leader, your job is not about producing widgets. Mostly it's about people. It's about giving them the tools they need to produce the widgets. This means you have to make time in each day to talk them, to listen to what they have to say, and to be aware of who they are and what they do.
2. *Keep it simple.* Having agreements and knowing how people are progressing on an ongoing basis allows for a simpler, more accurate and much more satisfying performance appraisal.

In the end, if you were to lead and coach your team every day and manage your time accordingly, I believe performance appraisals in their current, generally distasteful form could be rendered unnecessary. I, for one, would celebrate that.

Leadership in these times calls for resilience and for recognizing what kind of guidance is needed and when. Mentoring and coaching, along with the other activities mentioned, provide the infrastructure that allows you as a middle leader to develop that resilience and nurture it in others.

THINK ABOUT IT

Q.Who are your mentors? How has having them in your life helped you?

Q. If you can't think of anyone who has mentored you in a more traditional sense, what about mentoring moments? Who has opened a door for you at some time in your life that might otherwise have remained shut?

Q. How important is mentoring others to you? Why? As well as the satisfaction that comes from sharing your knowledge and experience, what does mentoring someone do for you?

Q. As a middle leader, you are probably required to complete performance appraisals on those who report to you. How do you make it a useful exercise? What could you do more of to make the time you spend on this task more meaningful for everyone on your team?

NOTES

8

COLLABORATION

> *When I was a kid, there was no collaboration: it's you with a camera bossing your friends around. But as an adult, filmmaking is all about appreciating the talents of the people you surround yourself with and knowing you could never have made any of these films by yourself.*
>
> STEVEN SPIELBERG

In these days, there are few singular heroes. The red capes and suits with red S's on the chest are the stuff of fiction. While there remain some folks who believe their accomplishments come solely from their own efforts, more have come to appreciate that great outcomes are only possible with the contribution of others.

Collaboration has become a watchword for success in the twenty-first century. But what does it mean?

Randy Nelson, once the Dean of Pixar University, described it as "co-operation on steroids." I describe collaboration more specifically as *the act of working with another, or others, to create something that goes beyond the ability of any one person to produce.*

Successful collaboration doesn't seem to come easily to adult human beings who, in Western society anyway, seem to place greater value on competition and individual achievement. So, we have to work first on appreciating its value and then on doing the things necessary to ensure that, in the end, everyone involved gains the sense of accomplishment that we all crave.

How might you encourage people in your workplace to take a more collaborative approach to work or build on the skills they already have to accomplish your goals together?

Clarity of Purpose

It's unwise to assume that everyone involved is clear about the goals to be achieved. So job one is to ensure clarity of purpose. We talked about this in Chapter 3: Leading on Purpose. As a middle leader, you have to establish your own clarity first before you pass the word along to those in your charge. If in doubt, ask questions of your bosses and peers until you are satisfied you know your area's part in achieving the greater goal. Then you're in a better position to help your team to get clear on what is to be done.

Clarity of purpose also includes ensuring that those involved have a shared understanding about a couple of other things:

- why the work and the achievement of it is important
- what working together in a common interest can accomplish that working out of self interest cannot

In my experience, the *why* of it is much easier to explain to people than the idea that *working together* to accomplish something can be just as rewarding, or even more so, as achieving something alone. Organizations seem to *talk* a lot about working collaboratively but continue to fashion their reward systems to disproportionately acknowledge individual effort. If this is the case in your organization, this likely makes it tough for you to beat the drum for collaboration. As a middle leader, designing more expansive reward systems for your organization is probably not in your current wheelhouse. Still, this doesn't have to defeat you.

Using your influence to broach subjects of this nature (as well as other controversial subjects) certainly *is* in your wheelhouse as a middle leader. Indeed, if your organization's reward system is an obstacle in achieving your goals, it is your job and the job of those to whom you report, to do something about it. In the meantime from your place in the middle, there may be other ways to acknowledge group effort that don't require a major shift in policy. Such rewards, whatever you choose them to be, should appeal intrinsically to its participants and give them a sense of deeper satisfaction from working together. Although often less tangible, they are only limited by your imagination and where you choose to place your focus as the leader. So celebrate and reward the small wins together in whatever way will galvanize the collective effort and provide incentive to keep going.

You may ask, what does great collaboration look like when it's in action? Those who successfully encourage and practice collaboration do six things well.

1. *Engage in and value conversation.* They take an interest in others. In fact, they use conversation as a simple yet effective way to learn about others and the potential they may have for working well together in collaborative efforts.
2. *Find ways to draw out creativity in themselves and others.* No idea is discounted or censored, just played with until it either becomes something bigger, or fizzles out. At Pixar University, they use improvisation as a tool for opening doors to new ideas and perspectives. Others use a variety of brainstorming techniques.
3. *Actively seek self-knowledge and learning.* They use their curiosity as a tool to explore and discover new possibilities. Those who know what they're good at and enjoy also know how they can make their best contribution to the collaborative effort.
4. *Invite contribution and accept what is offered without judgment.* Those who collaborate productively choose to build on what others offer through ideas, questions, and discussion. They resist the temptation that catches so many of us: to first look for flaws when another offers an opinion or a piece of work.

5. *Make others look good.* This simply means focusing on the work and the contributions others make before seeking personal recognition.
6. *Manage disagreement well.* While we might like to think that effective collaboration is void of disagreement, it isn't. Those who are skilled collaborators see the value in the tension that disagreement can produce and use it as a bridge to get to something different, or something better.

The Value of the Dissenting Voice

The truth is, although the word *collaboration* can conjure up images of people working happily together, I rather think we would get closer to reality if we included a few arguments, some eye-rolling and some exasperated, over-emoted sighing to round out the picture.

Mostly, this kind of friction happens because, as individuals, we differ from each other in culture, experience, and skill. The perspectives we hold come from those things. And, as human beings, we stubbornly cling to them, shutting out the possibility that there may be another way. Yet, if we want to truly extract the best ideas and create the best outcomes, we must be prepared to include the likelihood that our view is not always going to be the best. That means making room for the friction created by those who look at things through a different lens and having the courage to share what they see.

I don't know about you, but at times I have discounted the opinions of others because their logic sounded wrong or what they were saying had, in my view, no bearing on the matter at hand. In those situations, I wonder what might have happened had I spent just a few more minutes listening and trying to understand. Of course, there was always the possibility that what was being said was complete drivel. But, it was equally possible there was something there of great value that was lost because I failed to take the time to really listen.

In a world where time is at a premium, the behaviour I describe above is not unique. So many of us spend our days striving to get to the end, or accomplish a goal, and yet sacrifice the quality of what we produce by ignoring the voices that don't seem to have a place on our personal radar screens.

There are lessons here, regardless of whether we need to make room for the dissenting voice or we *are* the dissenting voice.

- *Develop a discipline of drawing out those who may be reluctant to speak.* Some people can feel overpowered by the common opinion. In fact, they may believe their own view to be less important because it is different. And so they stay quiet so as not to rock the boat. Drawing them into the conversation can make it more real and provide the opportunity for a wider variety of ideas to be shared.
- *Provide enough time for reflection, curiosity, and discussion.* If you make room for the dissenting voice, you also must make time for people to ask questions, explore, challenge, and think about what is being said. It may take longer, but the conversation will be enriched because of it.
- *Give the dissenting voice a place at the table.* That means, when you come together to discuss some aspect of your collaboration, assign a virtual place for the dissenting voice. Over the course of your discussion, stop from time to time and invite people to place themselves in a perspective they may not currently hold. Sometimes this will give rise to a new idea that may not have otherwise surfaced. And it will encourage those who really do think differently to become part of the conversation.

When You Are the Dissenting Voice

Conversely, if you are in a similar meeting with your peers and/or bosses and you find yourself differing from the rest in experience, perspective, or opinion, honour the spirit of useful collaboration and be a role model for your direct reports. Here's how:

- *Find the courage to stand up and speak.* While it can be nerve-wracking to share an opposing view, it can also be very liberating. Little is accomplished by waiting until a meeting is over to voice an adverse opinion, to no one in particular. If you want to be counted, stand up and be counted. It matters.

- *Ask questions that provoke thought.* Sometimes a well-placed question can slow the momentum of a meeting long enough to allow thoughts to take a much needed detour. Questions that begin with, "What would happen if…?" Or, "How might X apply to this situation?" can spark ideas not yet explored.
- *Explain the relevance of your view to the subject at hand.* If your view represents a big departure from the prevailing thinking, you stand a better chance of having it heard if you explain how it connects with the subject under discussion and the value it brings to realizing a successful outcome.

 It is the man who does not want to express an opinion whose opinion I want.

ABRAHAM LINCOLN

From that I surmise that Mr. Lincoln was keen to be informed on many levels, to solve the right problems, and to make good decisions more often than bad ones.

Putting the Constructive into Criticism

As a leader, if often falls to you to steer people and the work they do in a direction that allows collaborative efforts to remain functional. This means that while the work of the group and the collective goals are paramount, you need to ensure the contributing individuals are each in a position to make their best contribution. Sometimes it also means you have to offer criticism.

Criticism may not be agreeable but it is necessary. It fulfills the same function as pain in the human body. It calls attention to an unhealthy state of things.

WINSTON CHURCHILL

I really think this is a good way to look at it, regardless of whether you are on the giving or receiving end of criticism. However, there is criticism...and then there is criticism.

Most leaders like to preface the word *criticism* with the word *constructive*. That makes its aim one of building rather than tearing down. Yet, not all carry out the *constructive* part well, which usually means the *criticism* part is prone to cause a deterioration in the state of things.

In your dealings with your own direct reports, or even with your peers and bosses, how might you make sure the criticism you deliver is going to be worthwhile enough for them to take on board and really consider?

Before you proceed to offer criticism, you must first put yourself under some scrutiny and examine whether you do indeed intend your criticism to be constructive. To do that, here are three questions to ask yourself.

1. *Why do I feel the need to criticize?* Criticizing constructively must carry with it an equally constructive purpose. If, for instance, your criticism comes out of anger, frustration, or another negative emotion, then you're using it to vent and not to help or make things better. So, first you must determine how your criticism might serve the person being criticized and to some extent improve the negative situation his or her behaviour has created.

2. *What, or who, am I concerned about?* Similarly, if expressing your criticism will make only *you* feel better, then you're probably doing it for the wrong reason. Caring about people you lead often includes pointing out things to them that they cannot see for themselves. In other words, the focus of criticism needs to be on enlightenment and not on wielding power over another.

3. *Am I prepared to listen?* When you offer criticism it is usually because you have a concern about someone's behaviour, performance, results, or a combination of all three. You draw conclusions based on what you observe, what you experience, and what others tell you. However, to make criticism useful to the person on the receiving end, they have to know that you

are willing to hear from them too. Otherwise, the information on which you base your judgment will be incomplete and in danger of being wrong, misconstrued, rationalized away, or ignored.

Beware the Crap Sandwich

Criticizing another person's behaviour or performance is not a *fake it 'til you make it* proposition. There are many ways to offer constructive criticism. Some recommend the crap sandwich approach: beginning with something positive, moving to the negative, and closing with something else positive. I'm not a big fan of this because, even with the best of intentions, using a prescribed method of delivery can come across as contrived and even condescending.

Empathy and sincerity are the only things that matter, even if the delivery is a little rough. My advice, when it comes to offering criticism to another, is to approach it with a caring heart and honest intent.

Collaboration and Servant Leadership

Some people will consider the notion of the servant leader as a fad that will go away if they ignore it. Others will make every effort to embrace it, but find themselves exhausted, confused, and resentful because other people seem to be walking all over them.

There are many synonyms for the word *servant*. In the thesaurus, wedged between the words *attendant* and *steward* (two perfectly benign offerings), I found the words, *lackey, flunky, minion,* and *drudge*. So, if there is a problem with the concept of servant leadership, it possibly lies in the way the servant is perceived. Serving, to some, means we are also submitting to the whims of others for no other reason than to render them superior. Let's face it, our egos are going to have a hard time with that.

However, there is a place for service in developing a collaborative environment and not just for the leader.

For instance, it is your role as a leader to keep everyone focussed on the goals to be achieved. In this way you serve the larger purpose. You also serve the individuals who are participants in the work by doing what is necessary to progress it. Sometimes that means rolling up your sleeves and working alongside the rest. Sometimes it means lobbying for resources and training. Sometimes it means challenging the status quo. Whatever the activity, you do it in *service* of getting the results you all want.

Where we can go wrong with the servant leadership thing is that we fail to expect all who are involved, be they a designated leader or a data input clerk, to serve too.

An environment that embraces service will do so in an all-encompassing way. This means that regardless of title or position, each person will both lead and serve another, or group of others, to attain company goals and make a contribution to the achievement of its purpose.

To do this, you will be required to call on three principles that can be greatly undervalued in circumstances where collaboration is critical. They are humility, trust, and faith.

Humility

Humility is about putting others before yourself. It's a challenge, especially in business where individual competition is a large part of working life. However, for collaboration to succeed there must be a measure of selflessness that allows you to listen and consider the needs of others and their contribution to the work.

Trust

Trust is earned. However, a leader in service mode will start from a platform of trust rather than skepticism. In my experience, people respond well to a leader who conveys belief in them and in their good intentions. People who feel trusted are more likely to be eager to do well so as not to disappoint. Will you be disappointed? Yep. Sometimes. But if you start out by not trusting, my hunch is you're going to be disappointed anyway and probably a lot more often.

Faith

I'm talking about the kind of faith that makes you believe so strongly in what you're doing and the people you're doing it with that all your energy and activities stay focussed on that. With that kind of intensity, the results will speak for themselves.

The Bottom Line

However difficult it may be at times, collaboration has become a necessary and valuable part of working life. Whether you are engaged in a for-profit, non-profit, or voluntary effort, your ability to work together with others in the pursuit of a common purpose will define your success. As a middle leader you have an opportunity to play a significant role in shaping your organization's approach to working collaboratively.

So, keep focussed on the goal. Reward group effort whenever you can. As irritating as it may be at times, appreciate and value the dissenting voice. Work with your peers and bosses to create and sustain a collaborative environment, even (or perhaps especially) if it means being the dissenting voice. Put the constructive into your criticisms in service of making things better. And serve the collective purpose in any way you can.

THINK ABOUT IT

Q. What does collaboration look like to you when it's working well?

Q. How close are you to that ideal in your own workplace? What is the evidence—what you are seeing and experiencing—that makes you confident in your assessment?

Q. As a middle leader, what can you do to help move your team and your colleagues closer to achieving your ideal collaborative environment? How might you use this to influence the greater organization?

Q. Who most often provides the dissenting voice in your regular discussions at work? How have you responded to that person (or those people) in the past? If you agree now that the dissenting voice can serve a very useful purpose in achieving optimal results, what could you do differently to maximize its usefulness?

Q. What else might you do to get better at collaborating? Why would you want to?

NOTES

9

LEADING TEAMS

 Coming together is a beginning. Keeping together is progress. Working together is success.

HENRY FORD

I n working life, the word *team* seems to roll off our tongues quite easily. When hiring new people, advertisers rarely fail to ask for *team players*. We refer to the people who work for us as *our team*. Maybe we use it so liberally because the word itself has a warm glow of inclusion about it, but in truth, saying you are a team and being a team is not the same thing.

A Team That Wasn't

There was once a meeting in a company boardroom somewhere in a great metropolis. All the wise people sitting around the table decided it would be a good idea to form a team to undertake an important process improvement project. So they asked the company CEO to take charge of it.

After the meeting, the CEO summoned a few of his most trusted advisors, each from a different area of the company. In combination, they chose twelve people who might work together to come up with process improvement recommendations that the CEO could take to the board for the next quarterly meeting. The project was affectionately named the PIP, for process improvement project.

To make sure of an executive presence on the PIP, they appointed one of the advisors, a vice-president, to oversee the work and act as team sponsor. Her name was Carla. Carla was a very busy woman. The last thing she needed was another team to preside over. But you know the old saying: If you want something done, give it to a busy person. So, Carla put aside her doubts and decided she could squeeze this added assignment in somewhere. Besides, it might look good on her resume.

The selection process for the team was pretty simple. Carla, the CEO, and each of his other advisors chose his or her best and brightest to be a team member. Their criteria for choosing members was unclear except that each person chosen had been recognized as having high potential and had distinguished themselves in some way. And so it was assumed that bringing them together would result in a very productive, even powerful outcome. It was a great beginning.

Then came the day when the group of twelve met to talk about how they were going to proceed with the PIP. Carla attended this meeting for the first fifteen minutes. During this time she quickly gave the group its mandate for the project and some general idea about what was expected when it was complete. She asked for questions and, receiving none, expressed her confidence in the team's ability to work together. Then she left, in a hurry to get to her next appointment, promising she would look in from time to time to see how the PIP team was doing.

For the next few minutes, the PIP team sat in silence, somewhat stunned by the whirlwind that was Carla and by the seeming ambiguity of the assignment. Soon, they began to talk. Each member had a different idea about how to get started. However no one could hear anyone else over the din of the collective discordant voice.

No one was designated as leader of the team as they all felt equal in status and saw no need for a leader. After all, they had Carla. They decided not to waste time talking about roles and responsibilities within the team because they were adults, after all, and would rely on reason, logic, and common sense to guide their actions and decisions.

The PIP team met weekly. It seemed while they were getting to know each other there was a hierarchy developing among them. Those who made the most noise got the most attention. Those few members who enjoyed higher profiles in their day-to-day jobs (a.k.a. the rock stars) showed less commitment to matters of process improvement because, after all, that was for the back-room folks.

Others, who were genuinely interested in the project and could see some value in the work, seemed unable to attract enough attention away from what was *not* working to point out the possibility of what *might* work. As well, Carla's intention to attend meetings and provide guidance proved a disappointment. Her workload was such that she was often out of the office, indeed out of the country, and her phone was perpetually on voicemail.

Needless to say, the work of the PIP team floundered as team members became frustrated and overloaded with not only the worry of the project but also keeping up with their normal daily responsibilities. Due to other commitments, a few of the members left the team and were replaced. There was no time to bring the newbies up to speed. They were expected to get there on their own as quickly as possible.

Then, amid the chaos one day, Tony decided it would be a good time for him to take over. Tony was a senior manager who had some pretty strong opinions about how the PIP should be managed. He was sick of spending so much of his time treading water. He had better things to do. Without consulting the rest of the PIP team, he decided to cut everyone else out of the process by drawing up his personal recommendations and, on his own, presenting them to Carla, thus hijacking the team and what little progress it had managed to make.

When the other team members heard what Tony had done, they were flabbergasted. Half of the recommendations he had made bore no resemblance to the matters they had discussed and agreed on in their meetings. A few rose up in righteous indignation. But mostly, by this time, they were all so tired of trying to make things work, there was a secret thread of relief coursing through their veins. But there was no feeling of accomplishment. That was for certain.

None of the team members ever heard what happened to the project or its findings. It seemed to them to have been swallowed up by the tide of More Important Things or lost in the deep recesses of Carla's briefcase.

And, what was meant to be a highly functional team turned out to be a group that never quite managed to become a team at all.

But what might this group have been able to say if they *had* been successful as a team? Maybe something like:

EVERYONE ON THE TEAM CLEARLY UNDERSTOOD ITS PURPOSE.

While it may seem a bit obvious, it would appear that The PIP team spent almost no time reaching agreement on why they were together and what they were expected to produce. Carla's brief appearance did little or nothing to reinforce the team's purpose, gain commitment from its members, or clarify her own role in supporting its efforts.

It is always wise to make sure that the purpose and objectives of the team are commonly understood before starting anything else. It might take a little extra time and patience to get there, but failing to gain this kind of clarity can result in people running around like chickens in a yard, clucking loudly yet producing little.

INDIVIDUAL TEAM MEMBERS KNEW THEIR ROLES IN THE FULFILLMENT OF THE PURPOSE.

When we form teams, we presumably do so with some idea as to how each member can contribute. The PIP team members were chosen in a less than scientific way. That is, they each were high performers in their own area of work. However, when building a team, look beyond what people have historically produced and focus instead on the skills that allowed them to produce it. Different teams require different skill sets depending on their purpose and expected results. A group of high-functioning, high-potential people does not necessarily guarantee the best team results if they are not placed in roles that play to their strengths. For instance, it might have been a good idea for the PIP team to designate someone to lead its meetings, perhaps someone with facilitation skills whose strengths in keeping the team focussed on the task would serve it and its purpose well.

INDIVIDUAL TEAM MEMBERS SAW THEIR ROLES AS NO MORE IMPORTANT THAN ANY OTHER.

A true team does not involve hierarchy. Yes, there may be a team leader, but the role of the leader is no more important than anyone else's when it comes to fulfilling the team's purpose. In short, the work becomes more important than any individual's need to be, or be seen as, the boss.

THEY PAY ATTENTION TO THE TEAM DYNAMIC EVERY TIME A NEW MEMBER IS INTRODUCED.

The nature and culture of a team is somewhat of a sensitive thing. Each time a new member is introduced, the dynamic of the team changes. The PIP team virtually ignored the presence of its new members and allowed the team no time to adjust to the shift in circumstance. It would have been wise, on point of entry, for the team to conduct a general review of everyone's role, skills, and potential contribution. It didn't need to be a long drawn-out process, simply a realignment of roles to ensure the best possible results.

In the end, because the PIP team was unsure of its purpose, unclear of individual roles within the team, and lacked commitment from its sponsor and likely some of its members, work it eventually produced proved lacklustre.

When Teams Fulfil Their Purpose

Normally, when a team has fulfilled it purpose, it disbands. However, it's not unusual for it to be repurposed and move on to produce other things. In this way, teams can stay intact for a long time, transforming as new people join and others leave.

When you think about your own experience either leading a team or being part of one, it may help you to watch for the presence of purpose, defined individual roles, changing dynamics and focus on results that will fulfil the purpose. As well, when a company puts a team together, it owes the team commitment and support. It seems to me that no matter how big or complicated the team is, to function capably these elements have to be present. Otherwise it's probably a group.

And while you don't have to be a member of a team to accomplish good things, it takes more than just saying you're a "team" to make it so.

Having gone through a scenario that illustrates where teams can fail, let's look at one that *has* to get it right because lives depend on it.

The Snowbirds

The Snowbirds, officially known as the *Canadian Forces 431 Air Demonstration Squadron,* are a precision flying team. Apart from putting on a pretty spectacular air show, they offer clear confirmation of what can happen when you get collaboration and teamwork right.

In addition to being clear about the team purpose and his or her role within the team, each member of the squadron comes to understand and rely on the other members to ensure excellent performance and optimal safety.

The approach to the makeup of the squadron is taken seriously. In fact, choosing their team members carefully is critical. Their decisions must include precise specifications about skill, experience, values, behaviour, and potential because making a poor choice when recruiting team members has the capacity for a disastrous result.

With respect to hierarchy, you may note that the military is rife with rank and protocol. However, when it comes to the operation of the Snowbirds Squadron, rank is observed and respected while working on the team principle that those on the ground are as important as those in the air. In most organizations there are those who are more visible than others. These are the stars, the ones who are highly skilled in one particular area of the team's work. It's easy to assume that these people *are* the team. However, the Snowbirds pilots can only fly if they have the benefit of the skill and knowledge provided by those on the ground.

There are nine CT-114 Tutor jets in the Snowbird fleet. Each plane has its own dedicated technician who ensures his or her plane will fly safely and at peak performance for the pilot. In other words, nine pilots in the air cannot do their jobs safely or well without the support of the ground crew and the rest of the team—no matter how skilled a pilot might be.

In the Snowbird Squadron, the team is always changing. However, it manages the dynamics of change in an evolutionary way. Each pilot is assigned to the squadron for three years. After that, he is reassigned. The turnover is planned in such a way that the more experienced pilots play a role in the orientation and training of the new ones. In this way, the team continues to grow in depth and maturity while keeping the experience fresh for everyone.

There are many kinds of teams but no matter how complicated or simple, trust is the glue that binds highly effective teams together. I think it safe to say that when it comes to high precision flying teams like the Snowbirds, the absence of trust would keep them all grounded. This is also true of teams in other organizations. Finding ways to build trust and taking the time do it are crucial activities no matter where you sit in the company organization chart. Even with the noblest purpose, the best team members and the finest resources, if there is no trust, there is no team.

As a middle leader you are probably involved with teams all the time. You may have recognized something in the story of The PIP team or the story of the Snowbirds in your own experience. Hopefully you will also have picked up a few tidbits about what makes a team functional and how it can become dysfunctional. In the end, teams are only as good as the people who participate in them.

Edith and the Final Word on Teams

Edith was a clerk among a myriad of others working in the international department of the very large bank that employed us both. Back then, I was a personnel officer, although it was a role much more akin to police officer than anything else. And Edith was a pain in the neck.

She was notorious for not showing up for work on Fridays. Long weekends seemed to suit her, much to the chagrin of her manager. Her excuses were priceless.

Once, when asked about a Friday absence, she remarked, "Well, on

Thursday I went to the cafeteria for lunch and they were serving fish. They only ever serve fish on Friday. Naturally, I thought Thursday was Friday, so the next day, thinking it was Saturday, I didn't come in."

All the time I worked with Edith, I thought her to be an often cantankerous, rather silly woman. In my youth and to my shame, I looked down on her. Her job performance was not particularly remarkable and her eccentricities, of which there were many, were a source of both amusement and great irritation.

Edith retired at the mandatory age of sixty-five. She went happily into the sunset without my, or her manager, ever really understanding who she was or what we might have learned from her. That kind of thing happens when you're arrogant, when you look at people not as people, but as employees... bums on chairs.

Recently, I happened upon Edith's obituary. She died in her ninety-seventh year. She was a woman who had endured hardship all her life. When she was very young, she suffered a complete memory loss, something that even the strongest among us might have difficulty coping with.

In her middle age, while also working for the bank, she was caring for an erratic mother and living in a farmhouse with no electricity, heating, or indoor plumbing.

Later, she married a man who was a refugee, someone who had lost his entire family in Europe during World War II.

Together, they worked to acquire property, without incurring debt. They did this through, as described in the obituary, a shared philosophy of *mend and make do*. In the end, this approach helped them amass a winter home in Florida, a family home in Toronto, and some acres in Muskoka.

So what is my point? A team is made up of people. It is the leader's job to learn as much as possible about what those people are capable of bringing to it and to encourage their willingness to do so.

Had I, or her manager, stopped for just a little while to look deeper, beyond Edith's dowdy appearance and eccentric ways, we might have seen a creative woman with great business sense and a steely determination to achieve her goals. We might also have seen someone capable of fierce loyalty and resilience... all skills that any team would be glad of.

But we didn't. And our opportunity to capture Edith's attention and draw from her experience was lost. Instead, the performance she gave at the bank can only be described as sufficient unto the day, a means to an end. She didn't care because we didn't care.

So if you think that seeking depth as well as breadth in the relationships you build at work is just a warm and fuzzy thing to do, I invite you to think again. There is gold to be mined beneath the surface. What you find could be more than useful in helping you build a focussed team bent on achieving its business goals.

As for Edith, she may or may not have responded differently had we behaved differently toward her. But we'll never know, will we?

THINK ABOUT IT

Q. How important is real teamwork in your workplace? Why does it matter?

Q. If you were asked to define *team* in the context of your workplace, what words would you use? How do these words fit with concepts presented in **In the Thick of It**?

Q. What words would you like to be able to use to describe your team?

Q. If, like the Snowbirds, teamwork is integral to the success of your workplace, how might your organization increase its team effectiveness?

Q. As a middle leader, what part of improving team effectiveness belongs to you? What have you done so far? What's next?

NOTES

SECTION IV: LEADING THROUGH CHANGE

10

THE CHALLENGE OF CHANGE

 Change is inevitable except from a vending machine.

ROBERT C. GALLAGHER

Of all the challenges thrown at you as leader in the middle, coping with change and leading others through it has got to be the most difficult. Periods of calm and stability have become a rare thing, supplanted by perpetual motion as technology advances and the impact on our economy gain speed like a snowball in an avalanche.

In this chapter we'll talk about how you, as middle leader, can navigate the waters of planned and unplanned change, helping your team to rise above the challenges inherent in change and to meet both the business and human needs of your organization. We'll talk about what's different about planned versus unplanned change, what's the same, and we'll talk about the things you want to ensure you incorporate into your leadership tool kit: autonomy, mastery, purpose, innovation, and creativity.

The Challenge of Unplanned Change

We can be going along quite happily and then, bam, something unexpected happens that changes everything. I call these times "potholes." Some people hit more of them than others, for reasons only known to the cosmos. But whether there are few or many, whether they are shallow or deep, hit them you will.

It happened to me one day in 2009. I was happily remarried, retired, and living reasonably carefree. My husband and I were eating dinner one summer's evening, enjoying each other's company over a lovely glass of wine. At the end of the meal, he got up from the table to clear the dishes. As he was at the sink, starting to load the dishwasher, I heard a little noise. It was the noise you make when you take in air too fast. I asked him if he was all right.

"I'm really dizzy," he replied.

I turned around and saw him leaning over the sink, gripping the counter top as if to keep from falling over.

I quickly moved a kitchen chair behind him. He sat down heavily, but didn't seem to be able to let go of the counter top. He said the room was spinning and he felt sick. And then his speech began to slur, and the left side of his face to droop.

I called 911.

We waited an agonizing length of time for the paramedics to come. In truth, it wasn't that long. It only felt like forever. I stood beside him while we waited, uselessly massaging his shoulder and feeding him platitudes about how everything was going to be all right. But I didn't know. What's more, no one knew.

This wasn't the first stroke my husband had endured. The first one had occurred eleven years earlier. Through luck and a lot of hard work, he had made a nice recovery from that, regaining about ninety-five percent of his pre-stroke mobility and experiencing no discernible cognitive deficits.

This one was different. A blood clot had lodged itself at the base of his brain. Surgery was necessary to remove it but it had done its damage and ensured that while he was to survive, his life would never be the same. Nor would mine.

Change is often like that: sudden, scary, and unwelcome. As individuals, we live on fairly neutral ground, with fluctuations created by intervals of great joy and profound sadness. As a middle leader, and also an individual, you will be familiar with the questions and doubts that pass through your mind when contemplating your current situation and what is to come next.

You may ask:

Am I on the right path?

Am I doing enough?

Am I enough?

Do I need to change something? If so, what?

What would happen if I changed nothing?

I think these are all reasonable questions, ones that may be born out of crisis, or not, but require answers if you're going to achieve clarity of purpose and help others do the same.

Leading Planned Change

Often, we're spared the smack upside the head of unplanned change. We can see it coming. Perhaps we're even making it happen, which means having some measure of control over how you approach it. It's helpful to remember that even though you may be in the driver's seat, or at least sitting up front implementing changes that were conceived somewhere in the hierarchy above you, these changes may well feel like unplanned changes to the people you are leading.

In the end, the success or failure of any planned change effort comes down to people. Certainly theories, processes, structures, methodologies, and technologies all play a role in determining the direction and mechanics of change. But it will be people who make it work.

It's reasonable to assume that as leader, your preference would be for people to embrace change and to accomplish it with enthusiasm and pride. But, like everything else, you'll have to work for it.

The Way We've Always Done It

At this point in your career, you will not be unaccustomed to change. You will also know that change, once instigated, may very well include a few crises. The road to something different will fluctuate from high ground to low, to neutral ground and back again, with crisis playing the role of pothole along the way. Changing something we know and are familiar with in favour of something we don't know and are unsure about is very tough.

Why is that? You may ask. I don't have the answer, except that most of us hate change and that's not a position limited to the human race. How often have you heard someone in your workplace respond to the question, "Why?" with the dreaded, "Because that's the way we've always done it."

Those who are brave enough to explore further by asking, "Yes, but why has it always been done that way?" rarely receive a satisfactory answer because the truth is, nobody really knows why.

You're nodding your head, aren't you? I'm not surprised. It seems to be a fairly common occurrence, especially in long-established companies. However, there may be an explanation for it in the story of the five monkeys. Now, it's not a true story, in that the scientists and the research didn't happen exactly the way the story is often told. But it does a good job of demonstrating the point.

The Five Monkeys

The story goes something like this. Scientists placed five monkeys in a cage together. In the cage they also placed a ladder and at the top of the ladder they put a bunch of bananas.

Every time a monkey went up the ladder, the scientists soaked the rest of the monkeys with cold water.

After a while, each time a monkey attempted to go up the ladder, the others would attack him. Once the attacking behaviour was established, the scientists stopped the water-hose treatment. Still, the monkeys would attack any other monkey attempting to make the climb. Soon there came a time when no monkey would dare to go up the ladder for fear of being beaten by the others.

It was then decided to take one monkey out of the cage and replace it with another. Of course, the first thing the new monkey did on arrival was to go up the ladder for the bananas. The others attacked him immediately.

Several beatings later, the new monkey had learned never to go up the ladder despite the enticing bananas waiting for him at the top.

A second original monkey was removed from the group and replaced by another new monkey. Predictably, this new monkey also made his way up the ladder for the bananas and received a beating for his efforts. Interestingly, the monkeys who attacked him included the first new monkey.

The replacement of each of the original monkeys continued until all had been substituted for a new one. These five new monkeys continued to attack any one of them who dared to try and climb the ladder, in spite of the fact that the original reason for avoiding it (the cold water shower), was no longer a threat.

If we were to ask them and they had the capacity to reply, it's likely their response would go something like, "I don't know. That's the way things have always been done around here."

As human beings we like to think we have evolved a little more and are not so easily manipulated as the monkeys in the story. However, the story illustrates how we can fall into patterns of behaviour without really understanding the reason. In organizations, we can also become so deeply entrenched in our way of doing things, attempts to change are often greeted with a metaphorical dousing of cold water.

Motivation and Mastery

In times of change, you'll have two main jobs as a middle leader: to keep yourself motivated and focussed on your change objectives and to motivate your staff to keep on contributing their best. According to Daniel Pink, there are three things that in combination will truly motivate people to do their best work. These are:

AUTONOMY: the freedom of people to, either independently or with others of their choosing, work creatively to produce something they can be proud of.

MASTERY: the opportunity for people to learn, grow, and build on their interests, knowledge, and abilities.

PURPOSE: (there's that word again) the need for people to connect to something greater than themselves, something they can believe in and strive to fulfil.

To create this atmosphere where autonomy, mastery, and purpose are the prevailing motivators, you must develop and nurture the art of leadership. You must know how to build relationships sufficiently to understand what those three things mean to each of the people under your charge and then work to bring out the best in them by means of whatever skill you can muster, using whatever intuition you have about human behaviour.

But what about during times of change? Ah. Great question. Autonomy, mastery, and purpose need to make friends with innovation and creative thinking to help support your team and your peers—possibly even your boss—in facing and adapting to change in the most functional way possible.

So, the question is: how do you invite innovation and creative thinking into your workplace even if others in your organization, including your peers and bosses, are in resistance mode?

First, look to your organizational values and how you translate those into the work you carry out in your own area of responsibility. Times may be changing but the principles and behaviours you value will likely not. As such, they can provide a measure of stability even if everything else that was once *normal* is bouncing around in the surf of uncertainty. So take the time to revisit your values and those of your organization. Determine how you might continue to honour them and use them to help you and those who follow you through the rough patches that change inevitably delivers.

When you invite innovation and creative thinking into your workspace you also, by association, invite challenge. This seems like a simple thing to do but sometimes egos can get in the way. For example, it's easy to fall into the trap of thinking you must have all the answers for those who question and challenge you. The truth is that you don't and you won't.

Inviting challenge into your workplace does not demean your role as leader. Indeed, it does quite the opposite, because challenge enhances the possibility of a fresher, more creative, and progressive outcome. That kind of leadership shows courage and places the emphasis where it belongs: on the work and the people who do it.

Failure as Part of the Process

I know we've talked about failure before. When it comes to times of change, failure is part of the process. There are lessons to be learned from it and while you won't try new things with the idea of failing, sometimes you have to try, and fail, before you can discover what really works. The real irony is that clinging to the familiar or doing things the way you've always done them will eventually lead you to failure anyway.

Finding ways to acknowledge people who put out fresh ideas, no matter how bizarre they may sound, demonstrates willingness on your part to embrace the possibility of change and the necessity for it in a time when change is the only thing you can collectively count on.

You may agree that the apple cart of stability is constantly being upset. You will not always know the *why* of everything but neither can you afford to accept things the way they are because that's the way you've always done them.

Back to Potholes

Potholes are equal opportunity conveyances to the land of change where we arrive unceremoniously and unprepared and where our first response goes something like, "Oh crap," or worse.

After my husband's 2009 stroke, the world I knew somehow looked and felt very foreign. I found myself sitting at the bottom of a very deep pothole, panicking, and wondering what to do next. There are always options but, at that red-hot moment, none was particularly attractive. So I just sat there and looked around to see what could possibly help me feel differently. It took some time, but soon some things emerged.

1. HOLES MAY BE DARK, BUT THEY DON'T LACK OPPORTUNITY. The truth is, if I hadn't landed deep in a hole, I might not have realized how much I like to write. In fact, with the exception of a dangling participle or two and some possible crimes against the laws of punctuation, I can write reasonably well. Also, from the confines of the hole, I have connected with some really remarkable people, people whom I might never have met in my "pre-hole" days. I learn from them regularly. What better way to get out of a hole than to grow out of it.

2. I'M TOUGHER THAN I THINK I AM. I guess we never really know what we're made of until we are plunged into a dark place and challenged to rise to the occasion. The bottom of a hole is a fearful place. It is fearful for me because it makes me question my ability to cope with what is being asked of me. The point is, most people are stronger than they imagine themselves being. So know that you are too.

3. JUST AS THERE ARE GREENER PASTURES, SO TOO ARE THERE DEEPER AND DARKER HOLES. On days when I feel resentful, or wishful, I'm often reminded of people who are in deeper holes and darker places than I will ever be. From this perspective, being in my particular hole doesn't look so bad and makes me feel a certain gratitude for being here instead of there.

4. NO MATTER THE DIMENSIONS OF THE HOLE, THERE IS ALWAYS LIGHT SOMEWHERE. Being in a hole made me think about my priorities. In the rush and anxiety of getting to the next thing, it is easy to lose sight of what is important. Sometimes, our circumstances will force us to go in directions we would not have chosen for ourselves. Remembering our basic values and focusing on them will guide us out of our respective potholes, help us get out of our own way and get moving again.

I didn't see it then, but it has been pointed out to me that my response to the very much unplanned stroke my husband suffered in 2009 has certain parallels to leading through change.

In particular, while I was likely as afraid as he was, something told me that staying calm would help us both, while panicking would not.

Panicking would also make it more about me. The situation required me to offer assurance in the face of loss and stability in the face of uncertainty. These are not uncommon demands in leadership. The good news is, even if you think you don't have the strength, my own experience suggests to me that you do. There is nothing particularly extraordinary about me. If I can do it, you can too.

Looking for Leadership

People look for leadership because they need clarity of vision, well-defined boundaries, guidance, and reassurance. In leadership, they need to find trustworthiness, credibility, and above all, courage. It is a tall order from one human being to another. After all, you may be a leader but in all likelihood you'll be sharing some of the doubt and as much of the pain that goes along with changing even when you fervently believe it to be the right move. This can be a lonely existence.

Leading from the middle through change means digging deep into your well of personal determination and perseverance in doing what you believe to be the right thing. Kind of like Norma Rae.

Norma Rae

Whenever I think of the challenge of change, I think of Sally Field. Well, not Sally Field exactly, but her character in the 1979 movie *Norma Rae*. I picture Norma, all five feet of her, standing on a table in the North Carolina cotton mill where she worked. On this particular hot day, with sweat streaming down her face, she stands alone on that table in protest, her arms held high, holding a sign that simply says, *Union*. She stands in defiance of her bosses, and on behalf of her frightened and reticent co-workers whose working conditions are appalling enough to threaten their health and livelihood. She does it because deep inside herself she knows it to be right. It's worth fighting for. It's worth the risk. It will make life better in the end. I notice her face as she's standing there. I see rebellion, fear, and desperation. And yet she stands there until the local police come and drag her away kicking and screaming.

That's the thing about change. It can be hard and scary and sometimes involves some kicking and screaming. That sort of change is rarely the kind we eagerly put our hands up for. That's when leadership and leaders are truly tested.

In times of change, the job of leadership requires the kind of grit that Norma Rae showed as she climbed upon her table and stood her ground. In such times, change means hard work, hard heads, hard times, and tender hearts. As a middle leader, this is what it's about. It's also about finding a way to embrace change while holding everyone who follows you to the promise of what achieving the change will bring with it. As such, you put yourself forward to be followed, challenged, criticized, and sometimes even scorned. It may require you to stand on your own metaphorical table with the dream of better, or maybe just different, held firmly in your hands. And you hope it's enough to convince any naysayers it's worth the effort.

In the End

The effort you make to master the art of leadership, no matter how many you lead, will pay dividends. This kind of leadership, the kind that values every human being, engenders trust and loyalty. If you value stability you will find it in people who choose to stay the course with you and your organization through difficult times as well as good ones. They will know their part, contribute to the achievement of your collective goals and hold themselves accountable for delivering the results they promise. Will there be setbacks? Complications? Mistakes? Aggravation? Of course! But you will have accomplished something great simply by engaging those whose hearts and brainpower extend beyond the limitations placed on them by others. And it's entirely possible you will have created more leaders.

The failures, bumps, and potholes are all part of the shift from what is, to what can be. They will make you wonder at times why you ever thought it was a good idea to risk taking on a new challenge in the first place.

But you know why.

It is that feeling you get when you make it. This is what we all strive for and thrive on, the fulfillment that accomplishment brings. It will spur you on, make you want more, and reaffirm your belief in yourself. This lies at the summit of your mountain and is the high that confirms the worthiness of your struggle.

THINK ABOUT IT

Q. I expect that as an adult human being you have experienced the smack-up-the-side-of-the-head kind of unplanned change. What have you learned from those times that will be useful to you when you are leading others through a planned change? How will it serve you?

Q. What three things might you do to encourage the development of autonomy, mastery, and purpose among those you lead?

Q. What opportunities might you have to collaborate with your peers and bosses in encouraging people to do their best work through the lens of autonomy, mastery, and purpose?

Q. In order to lead a group of others through a planned change, what do you need more of? What will it take for you to get it? What might you need to discard?

NOTES

11

KNOW THYSELF

 I yam wot I yam and that's all that I yam.

POPEYE THE SAILOR

Y ou could say that Popeye has attitude. His simple approach to self-knowledge shows little evidence of an examined life. It's a take-me-as-I-am-or-not-at-all proposition. And while you have to admire his confidence, it's not helpful if you are about to lead others through a sea of change. As a middle leader and a real-life human being, it's just not a luxury you can afford.

Why is self-knowledge important in times of change? Indeed, why is it worth pursuing at all? After all, the process of self-examination can be tedious, humbling, and exhausting. The thing is, at the same time you're leading others through change events, you're also experiencing change on a personal level. Be it planned or unplanned, you'll embark on the same emotional rollercoaster as the people you are meant to lead. Because of this, you will need to be acutely aware of your own responses and your impact on others. This knowledge will allow you to shepherd your personal reactions in a way that works for you rather than against you.

In this chapter we'll discuss the value of self-awareness when contemplating leading others, especially in times of change. We'll acknowledge some truths about being a middle leader in changing circumstances and offer some thoughts about improving self-awareness and managing emotions.

To Thine Own Self Be True

Someone once said to me, "You're always sitting on the bench watching, never in the game."

I like to think the remark was meant to be constructive, but it shook my sense of self. Did I really do that? Was I really just an observer of life and not a participant? The thought filled me with a sense of inadequacy and guilt that I carried around for some time.

I began to observe myself and watch for signs I was being a bystander. The idea just didn't seem to fit with my intuitive understanding of myself.

It's true that I have never been particularly adventurous. Growing up, when others were diving off high places into bodies of water or shushing down mountains on skis and snowboards, I was content to watch with admiration and awe as they tested their physical boundaries and pushed themselves to the edges of life. Was this me bench-sitting? But then it occurred to me that engaging in physically challenging activity is only one way of participating and experiencing growth. I did come off the bench, in other ways, to meet my own challenges and grow.

Growth happened at age forty, when I decided it was time to see what I was made of and to move three thousand miles away from my family and familiar surroundings .

Growth happened at forty-two, when I went back to school, a place where I had never felt particularly comfortable, to find out if I really was too dim to learn new things.

Growth also happened when I stood my ground in the face of disapproval from my boss and some of my colleagues and when I worked to change that disapproval to acceptance.

As for bench-sitting, as a leader, colleague, and a person with bosses, I began to see the value in my ability to observe: ask good questions, assess group dynamics, and accurately summarize what was going on in meetings. I worked well with groups and helped them keep the bigger picture in view when making decisions. In other words, while I was never going to do well overtly leading a charge, I had come to know that from my bench I could contribute just as well as the person whose presence was more visible as an active and aggressive player in whatever game was underway at the time.

It took me some time to recognize this in myself. But when I did, the notion that I was simply an onlooker in the game of life dissipated and I began to use my skills more purposefully and with greater confidence.

This is what I mean about self-knowledge working *for* you rather than against you.

Science and Self-Knowledge

There are scientific tools available that will provide some answers to the "who am I?" question. For instance, I quite like the Myers-Briggs Type Indicator. I like it because it allows a participant to choose their personality type rather than be pigeonholed by a testing process. I also like it because, in my experience, it is eerily accurate when helping someone self-identify. There are also tests associated with determining levels of emotional intelligence, or EQ, which has eclipsed the popularity of the IQ tests that were in vogue in workplaces for much of the twentieth century.

Scientific testing is good and useful to the extent that it hints at how well you are likely to cope in real circumstances. It can help you identify areas where you can build strength and confirm some things you already know. No doubt some tests are more accurate and more scientific than others. What they cannot deliver is a complete view of you and who you really are. Only you can do that. Even then, life will introduce things that cause you to change that view. You are not the sum of your test results or the values that others may place on them. You are the sum of your experiences and choices. These experiences serve to shape your values, opinions, and to some extent your vision of the future. What it takes to determine all of this is some time in self-reflection. Even if it doesn't come easily to you, I invite you to spend just a little time sitting on the bench... next to me.

Keeping it Real

Let's say you've spent some time on the metaphorical bench figuring things out about you. Now, with heightened awareness and confidence, you're ready to step up, get focussed outside yourself, and get on with helping others to adapt to changing circumstances. Sounds good, doesn't it?

However, knowing yourself and how you affect others on a deeper level is only a start. You know that as a middle leader there is a lot of pressure to be many things to many people. Some of this pressure comes from your own desire to please. Some comes from expectations placed upon you by your peers and bosses.

Be careful that this pressure doesn't make you try too hard for things that are either not possible or unhelpful to you in your quest to be a good, authentic leader—especially in times of change.

For instance, you may try too hard to be:

- *Popular.* I think everyone, to a greater or lesser extent, likes to be liked. But, trying too hard to be popular gets in the way of your ability to make tough decisions and to lead in a judicious way. People respect and respond well to leaders who are fair, much more than they respect leaders who focus on being popular.
- *Perfect.* If you strive for perfection you may also develop a tendency to micro-manage everything to death to avoid making mistakes. The trouble is, in so doing, you will more than likely annoy most everyone who works with you or for you. While it's admirable to want to do things well, it is not possible to get everything right all of the time. It's just not.
- *All-knowing and all-wise.* Leadership does not come with all the answers. It's too bad, but there it is. If you try too hard to create the impression you are the font of all knowledge, you are bound to disappoint and be disappointed. Besides, by

trying to answer every question, you'll be denying someone else an opportunity to search for his or her own answer.

- *Strong.* To some people, a leader should always be strong, impervious to the problems and worries that afflict other mortals. It's true that leadership asks you to bring your courage to work, it does not mean you can't share your concerns with others. Trying too hard to be strong places an unnecessary burden on you. It also excludes the possibility that others are willing and quite capable of helping.

If you do find yourself trying too hard, what can you do about it? Well, you can:

1. ACCEPT YOURSELF, WARTS 'N ALL

I think it helps to have a good handle on what you're good at and what you're not good at. It doesn't mean you should stop learning, growing, and improving... not at all. But having a certain confidence about who and *how* you are will give you permission to take the focus off yourself and onto others without having to try so hard.

2. EMBRACE THE IMPERFECT

I struggle with this one all the time but I keep working on it because when I attempt to achieve perfection, I invariably realize only frustration. Sometimes imperfect and done is better than perfect and incomplete.

3. LOOK AND LISTEN MORE... TALK LESS

When we try too hard there's a tendency to talk too much. While we're talking, we're missing the opportunity to observe and listen to others who may have better ideas. Including others' thoughts and ideas makes for a better outcome and will also take the pressure off you to have the right answer all of the time.

· · ·

4. Dare to be Vulnerable

Allow your humanness to come through and place more value on giving—and receiving—empathy. I think human beings are stronger when they allow each other a glimpse into what matters to them. Trying too hard to be strong and stand apart from the rest leads to isolation.

5. Lighten Up

Sometimes you just have to laugh. When you're trying too hard, it's entirely possible that you're also being way too serious. Laughing at ourselves can take the pressure and worry out of most situations. Wherever you go, take your sense of humour with you. It will serve you well.

The Perils of Emotional Stupidity

Leading others through change is tricky and stressful. When you lead from the middle, the sources of this stress are multi-directional.

This kind of stress can trigger behaviour your rational adult self would not generally find helpful and could leave you feeling somewhat foolish. Or worse.

Witness the time I was rearranging my home office. On that day, I experienced a particularly spectacular, um, brain fart. This tends to happen to me when attempting to work with anything electronic or mechanical for which I have neither aptitude nor patience.

Reorganizing the room required moving all of the computer equipment to another location, unplugging everything and then plugging it back in again. What could be easier? But somehow *I* got all mixed up among the various wires, plugs, power bars, and extension cords, and lost my internet connection.

Amid the mounting pressure, I fussed and fumed and completely lost my focus.

"Why won't the green light on the Airport Express thingy come on?" I demanded, to no one in particular.

I was discombobulated and increasingly upset that I was unable to figure it out. Eventually, I called the young man who had helped move the furniture and asked *him* for some thoughts. He coached me over the phone.

Were all my connections properly attached to the modem? Check. Were my extension cords viable? Check. And so it went, but to no avail.

Finally, he agreed to come over and take a look. He arrived with a new extension cord in hand (just in case), looked at my Airport Express thingy... and simply plugged it in. The internet connection was instantly restored. The result was one green light and one very red face.

To his credit, the young man did not laugh at me (well, not in my presence). And *I*, feeling very sheepish, could only laugh at myself. But it set me to thinking about the myriad of things that create pressure for leaders every day and how important it is to find ways to remain calm in the face of them. Looking back, I expect that had I not allowed myself to get into a complete lather, I might have noticed that the Airport Express thingy was unplugged. But I didn't... so I didn't.

This is a very simple story but it illustrates the importance of remaining calm even when you don't feel that way. As a middle leader it is especially important to be aware of the annoying things that prompt unreasonable responses in you. After all, *people will be watching*. What they see and experience from you could give them permission to conduct themselves in ways that align with your behaviour. So, if you allow yourself to get bent out of shape, it seems reasonable that others will allow themselves the same opportunity.

You will certainly have days when you feel snarky, miserable, angry, or otherwise out of sorts. It happens even to the saints among us. But your workplace is not the place to vent. If you do, chances are you will have bridges to build or repair and your plans for a smooth change transition will be in jeopardy.

How do you avoid this kind of emotional stupidity and stay calm when the pressures of the day start to pile up on you?

STOP AND TAKE A BREATH

If I had stopped and walked away for awhile and focussed on something else, I might very well have come back to the computer connection task with a mind clear enough and emotions settled enough to see what I was doing wrong.

NOTE YOUR TRIGGERS

I know that whenever I get involved with anything with wires or anything requiring assembly, I'm going to experience stress. It is a trigger for me. So, perhaps the next time I engage in work of this kind, I will bear it in mind and be a little more patient, not only with the task but also with myself. Noting the triggers that set us off has a way of minimizing frustration and the irrational behaviour that often stems from it.

MAINTAIN A SENSE OF PROPORTION

I don't know about you, but when I get stressed over something, it has a way of getting blown up beyond all reasonable proportion. Things that were a mere nuisance before somehow morph into something bordering on catastrophic. I'm thinking that I could avoid this in future simply by reminding myself that there is a solution to just about every problem and if *I* can't see it there is bound to be someone who can.

ENGAGE OTHERS IN PROBLEM SOLVING

Sometimes we just get too close to a problem to be able to see a way around or through it. This is when building relationships with others who are willing to help and advise us becomes very handy. Luckily, in my experience, people actually want to be a part of solutions. Often, it is just a case of asking them.

Emotional stupidity manifests itself in many ways. Some of the behaviour that comes from it is simply unproductive and often embarrassing. Other behaviour can be more destructive, destroying credibility and trust, which are hard earned and easily lost.

Could it happen to any one of us? We'd like to think not, of course. But, before we get too judgmental or complacent, let's remember the last time we leaned on our car horns and said some colourful things to the person a couple of cars away who just cut us off.

Being aware of your own triggers and managing them is important, not just for your own well being but to ensure that you do not sabotage your ability to build healthy relationships and lead others through changing times.

As a middle leader, guiding others through a successful transition from one thing to a new thing relies on your ability to know yourself first. It's kind of like putting the oxygen mask on your own face first during a turbulent flight.

It's not simply a matter of checking your personality traits or determining how emotionally intelligent you are. It's also about taking an inventory of the experiences you've had in your life thus far and determining how those experiences have shaped you and your attitudes.

Just as organizations change, sometimes drastically, sometimes almost imperceptibly, people too are always changing. You are never really going to know yourself so deeply that you could carve your image in stone and say, "This is who I am." But you can get close enough to trust and guide yourself through a change event—at the same time as you successfully lead others through it.

THINK ABOUT IT

Q. What do you know about yourself today that you didn't know ten years ago? Five years ago? Yesterday?

Q. In your experience, what have you found to be the best way to learn about yourself? How has it served you? What else might you try?

Q. When it comes to keeping it real, what do you typically try too hard to do? Like to be popular? Perfect? All-knowing? Strong like a lion? Something else? If it really gets in your way, what do you want to do about it?

Q. What makes you crazy? How do you typically react when something frustrates or annoys you at work? How does your reaction help overcome the problem? How does it mess things up for you? Knowing this, what must you change?

NOTES

12

BUILDING SUPPORT

 There is nothing more difficult to take in hand, more perilous to conduct, or more uncertain in its success, than to take the lead in the introduction of a new order of things.

NICCOLO MACHIAVELLI

You have no doubt faced both the planned and unplanned kinds of change. You know how they feel. You know, too, that while the process tends to be painful, it can also be exciting. And hopefully you'll know that feeling of satisfaction when you come out the other side intact and with a brand new "normal" that feels pretty good.

As a middle leader, change takes on another dimension as well. It's not just about you anymore. Also, while you may be prepared for it and have some idea what to expect, you can't assume that the people you lead are ready to follow you into new territory. This is because, as mentioned in Chapter 10: The Challenge of Change, your carefully-planned change could very well be a big old pothole for everyone else.

Even if you have enough authority to impose change in your area of responsibility, on its own, it will not be enough for people who work with you to want to follow you. For this, you need to build support.

In this chapter we'll talk about the two things you must earn and three things you must nurture within yourself that will help you build support for change and garner trust and confidence in your leadership. First, the two things to earn: credibility and trust.

Credibility

In general, people make a choice whether and when and who to follow. It doesn't matter whether you have the authority or the technical skill to pull off a change in a functional and positive way, if people choose to resist your leadership or *unfollow* you through other means, change will be difficult to execute. As such, earning credibility is a vital pursuit for any leader. It is credibility and not title, position, role, or authority that makes the difference between an effective change agent (a.k.a. you) and an ineffective one.

You must also earn credibility from your peers and bosses because they are part of the bigger picture. Indeed, the change you face will often have been decreed, or at least initiated, from on high. As such, their support for your efforts will be crucial to the success of the change you're managing. When your peers and bosses view you as a competent, reliable, believable leader, it is that much easier to do the work. Here's what it takes to earn credibility.

1. RELIABILITY

Do what you say you're going to do...and do it when you say you're going to do it.

Reliability is an important ingredient in establishing credibility. There's nothing more infuriating or counter productive than when someone makes a commitment to do something and then fails to follow through. This often means being diligent about what you say yes to. I know it can be tempting to agree to do something because you want to be a team player. However, if you say yes and you're unable to fulfill the commitment, the result is disappointment all around. And your credibility will take a hit.

. . .

2. HONESTY

Represent yourself honestly and do your best to be candid and open with your team, colleagues and bosses.

After doing the "know thyself" work from Chapter 11, it will be important to find the courage and confidence to simply be yourself and make your contribution without pretence or bravado. If you do this, your responses and contributions both in your conversations and actions will be consistent and reliable. That builds credibility.

3. FALLIBILITY

Show that you're open to learning and trying new things. Nothing will put holes in your credibility more than conveying the impression that you have all the answers.

Change is a learning experience in itself. If you go into it believing it's for everyone but you, you can't expect to influence change in others. They'll see right through it. Showing your curiosity, asking questions, and learning from mistakes are all part of the process. Rather than conveying weakness, doing these things openly demonstrates your willingness to learn and grow along with everyone else. It humanizes you as a leader and shows that you don't exist just to tell people what to do. It fosters more of a whole-team dynamic, rather than the autocratic or authoritarian dynamic more common in days gone by. It also demonstrates your commitment to change.

4. ACCOUNTABILITY

Own up to being human and making mistakes. And, when you do make them, apologize and do your best to make amends.

Making excuses for the mistakes you make is tempting but simply unproductive. You will not adversely affect your credibility when you make mistakes. You will adversely affect your credibility if you try to cover them up, rationalize them away, blame someone else or pretend they didn't happen in the first place. Enough said.

· · ·

5. RESPECT

Demonstrate respect for the experiences and knowledge of others. One of the best ways to build credibility is to observe those who have gone before you and learn from their experiences. The circumstances of their change event (or events) might differ from yours. Perhaps it happened in a different time with different tools available. But there is one thing that usually stays consistent and that is how human beings react to changes imposed upon them. Learning from others' experience no matter their role or rank will give you clues to what you can expect. If you want to be heard, you must first listen.

6. PROBLEM-SOLVING

When you challenge the status quo, you offer feasible and thoughtful alternatives. Presenting a problem without considering a solution is not supporting or driving change. It is simply complaining. When you go to your peers and bosses with a problem of some sort, be sure to have considered some possible alternatives. Doing this supports your credibility and also stimulates further exploration with a greater number of heads to work on solving the problem.

Trust

Trust is a small word. Yet it holds the key to every successful relationship, business venture, or change initiative. As I've said before, it's also hard-earned and easily destroyed, which makes it precious.

As a middle leader, you have many roles to fulfil. For you, the importance of building trust is paramount to your ability to influence upward, gather support from your peers, and guide those who follow you through changing times.

So how do you know when trust is present in your working world? What might you be seeing or experiencing in a trusting environment that is often missing in a workplace devoid of trust?

Here is when trust is present.

. . .

1. As a Boss.

As a boss, people are open and candid with you. They trust that you're not in the business of shooting messengers or punishing anyone for giving you straight and honest information about yourself, or anything else.

People working with you are not afraid to be creative or try new things. When they make mistakes, they own up to them and are willing to share their lessons with others.

As a boss, you strive for transparency in your dealings with others and that means you talk to them, ask their opinions, and listen to their advice. You feel well-rewarded and highly-regarded.

2. As Part of a Team

As part of a team, you don't waste time engaging in gratuitous political maneuverings. You focus instead on building solid and positive relationships with your colleagues for your benefit and for the team.

You fulfill your responsibilities to the team and the organization and take pride in both what you and the team produce.

You enjoy working together with your team, pitching in to do whatever work needs doing, even if it is technically not your job. You feel that you belong.

3. As an Individual Contributor

As an individual contributor, you are not afraid to ask questions, present your ideas, or challenge the status quo in the presence of your bosses.

You ensure you understand your role in the organization and if in doubt are quite comfortable asking someone who can teach you. If you have knowledge that a colleague needs but does not have, you don't hesitate to share what you know. You trust that sharing will give you and your colleagues all the power you need to get the work done well. You feel competent and important.

. . .

These scenarios are somewhat utopian. In many organizations the level of trust needs work. For example, I used to have a boss who hid around corners and pillars in the food court of our office building during the lunch hours, trying to catch people taking more than their allotted time for lunch. Oh, yes. While, hopefully, bosses who behave like that are rare, I expect you could recall your own version of a story that illustrates a time when trust was absent.

The point is, whether you are in the role of boss, team member, or individual contributor, there is opportunity for you to be instrumental in creating an environment that strives to build and maintain trust. If you work in a situation where trust levels are low, the work will be harder. However, the price of under-valuing the importance of the work or choosing not to do it at all is bound to be high and your chances of affecting positive change are diminished.

Three Things to Nurture

1. PATIENCE

Patience isn't often included in the list of primary attributes to look for in leaders. Yet it underpins good leadership. In a world where technology demands speed and the pressure to produce immediate results is all around you, cultivating the discipline to be patient is tough. In times of dramatic change it can be even tougher. Nonetheless, for you as a middle leader, it is a challenge worth pursuing. Here's why.

Patience will allow you to suspend judgment long enough to make considered decisions. Often, when the pressure is on, it's tempting to make snap decisions that you later come to regret. With a little patience, you can give yourself the benefit of stopping to consider the impact of the decisions you make and who you might be affecting. Ill-considered decisions usually result in having to take corrective action anyway, so there isn't any time savings regardless how you might feel in the moment.

Patience allows for late bloomers to develop. Not everyone learns or adapts at the same rate. In times of change this is especially true. Some, like the hare, will be quick out of the gate, while others, like the tortoise, will be slower off the mark. Each needs leadership to get to the finish line. Patience will require you to steer the hare and reach back to encourage the tortoise.

If you are a leader with little patience for the development of those who take more time to adapt than you'd like, you could be missing something. After all, Winston Churchill was a late bloomer.

Patience can help you to be a better listener. I think by now you recognize the value of listening, both to get to understanding and in building solid relationships. However, to accomplish either of those things there must be patience enough to suspend your own judgment and focus on what is being said rather than on what you are about to say.

Patience can help you manage stress. Getting to the place where you accept that sometimes you just have to wait can diffuse a lot of negative feeling. If you are frequently impatient with those around you, it is possible you are also frequently frustrated. Perhaps angry too. Managing your own expectations long enough to put matters into perspective can relieve a lot of tension and ultimately make work a more pleasant experience.

How to Develop Patience

- *Learn to value the questions as much as the answers.* This requires curiosity and exploration. Patiently peeling away the layers of a problem through questioning and listening results in a richer and more rewarding outcome.
- *Know the things that trigger your impatience and practice managing them.* Building from your work in Chapter 11: Know Thyself, focus on the triggers that make you snap, consciously practicing to extend your tolerance.
- *Keep the long-term goal in mind.* Change can be overwhelming and it's easy to get caught up in the pursuit of any short-term result. It will help you feel in control of something. However, if you spend all of your time chasing quick results, you can get sidetracked and lose sight of your larger change objective. Some opportunities are worth waiting for and some goals take longer to achieve. If they're

important, they deserve whatever time it takes to accomplish them.

In the final analysis, it's probably safe to say we all suffer from bouts of impatience, some more chronically than others. Impatience in leadership is particularly troublesome because it gets in the way of our ability to do the right thing at the right time. As a middle leader, you will not have control over how much patience your bosses and colleagues display but you can resolve to cultivate more patience in yourself and in your dealings with those who follow you.

It's true that patience is a virtue. I think it's also a discipline and one that every leader, no matter his or her standing in the organization, must develop to build support and ensure the success of any change project.

2. ATTITUDE...THE GOOD KIND

I used to spend a lot of time traveling for business, and while hotel stays became commonplace, certain attitudes from certain hotel staff stood out.

On one particular trip to Toronto, I stayed in a hotel that was, and is, a rather posh place to hang your hat. I found myself looking forward to the experience. Imagine my disappointment when I arrived to find an unmistakable chill in the air... and it wasn't the air conditioning.

The hotel porter, a tall, round, middle-aged man, looked distinctly unhappy. In truth, his attitude floated between us on a cloud of disdain as he escorted me to my room. When we reached our destination, he looked down his long thin nose and with an imperious sniff, unlocked the door to my room. Then he ushered me inside, somewhat like a naughty child, received his tip (what can I say? I caved) and closed the door swiftly behind me. Hmmm, I thought, not a good start.

Once *in* the room, I realized there was no hair dryer in the bathroom. And so I phoned housekeeping. The housekeeping department tersely informed me that while they would supply me with a hair dryer,

I would only be allowed to keep it in my room for half an hour. *Really?* This person didn't sound happy either. Nor was I.

In contrast, my husband and I once went on a short road trip to Vancouver, Washington. We stayed at a lodge-type hotel built to blend harmoniously with the Pacific Northwest environment. Here, we were warmly welcomed. The hotel staff was upbeat, positive, and friendly. I saw no miserable faces, no reluctance to serve, and no disdainful glances.

In the restaurant adjacent to the hotel our experience was even better. The wait staff was more than accommodating. And each morning at breakfast, Cecily greeted us with a cheerful smile. Cecily exuded happiness. She and the others, who all remained cheerful in spite of the busy breakfast period, helped us set our own moods for the day. People were happy. And so was I.

So what's the message here? It is that attitude rubs off for good or ill. Each hotel story suggests a culture that has dictated the prevailing attitude of its employees. Such attitudes come from the kind of leadership these employees experienced. As such, in your effort to affect change as a leader in your organization, know that your attitude toward it and the challenges you are going to face together will be absorbed like a thirsty sponge by those you lead. If you grumble, they will grumble. If you doubt, they will doubt. It's as simple as that.

Ensure your attitude is of the good kind. Find ways to get on board with the idea of the change project yourself before sharing contemplated changes with others. They will need your support and, most certainly, your empathy. If you need to grumble or doubt, take it to your boss and do it in private. Address your concerns. Challenge the process. Find your own clarity of purpose. Then, in your dealings with your own crew, you will be better equipped to engage them in change as a good thing, to listen to and allay their doubts and fears, and to work through the process in a functional and positive way.

3. FAITH

Faith. Canada is a secular society and "faith" isn't a word used a lot in the work environment here. It is an important word though, especially if you want to change something, achieve something, rise above something, or stretch beyond the boundaries of your current understanding.

The movie *Salmon Fishing in the Yemen* is a story about a wealthy Sheik who loves to fish. He wants to make it possible for salmon to live and thrive in Yemen, a place where water is scarce, so the people of Yemen can enjoy fishing. It seems like an impossible dream to everyone but him. And yet, he continues to pursue it and to believe in it. You could say he had the patience and the attitude to make his vision come to life. He also had faith in his chances for success and in his own ability to engage others in helping him turn what is possible into something real.

As a middle leader you know that leadership asks a great deal of you. It often demands that you strike out into the unknown and convince other people it's a good idea. It asks you to trust that some things do not come complete with scientific or rational explanation. It asks you, too, to believe in your own abilities: the potential and ability of those who work with you and in the value and viability of the vision you hold, even at times when that vision seems unlikely enough to be attainable.

Faith asks this of you but also makes room for great things to happen.

Faith allows you to step off cliffs. Being part of building and growing an enterprise requires you to take chances. Sometimes these are measured and well-researched and sometimes they constitute a leap of faith. The success of the latter often depends on how fervently you believe in your imagined outcomes. Those who doubt either themselves or their ability to bring the vision to reality are less likely to be successful.

Faith allows you to let go. When you place your faith in the ability and good intentions of others, you are free to concentrate on other important things. Of course, part of letting go includes successfully transferring the future vision to others. Once done it allows them the freedom to think, create, and produce great results in ways that you might not have imagined.

Faith allows you to see mistakes as reparable. When you really believe in what you're doing, mistakes become part of the learning and growing process. Indeed, if your faith in the direction you are taking is strong, the setbacks you inevitably experience will find a way of teaching you something useful.

Faith belongs in the workplace. It does not guarantee success but in times of change it allows for small, and sometimes very big, victories. And, like stepping stones in a stream, these victories eventually lead to the other side where you can look back and marvel at the journey. Maybe you can even go fishing in the Yemen.

So, building support for change starts with you. You may have the authority to change something, but authority on its own will not get the job done. Change is a people-centred process. To build support in changing times you must work to earn credibility, not only in the eyes of those who follow you, but also with your peers and bosses. Similarly, you must prove trustworthy in all you do.

Building credibility and trust often relies on your ability to be patient, check your attitude, and have faith, both in what you are doing to make things better, and in the people who work with you to accomplish it.

THINK ABOUT IT

CREDIBILITY

Q. When it comes to credibility, on a scale of 1-5 how would you rate yourself? If your rating is less than what you would like it to be, what has to happen for it to be better? What do you need more of? Or less of?

Q. If you were giving advice to a less experienced leader about earning credibility in your workplace, what would you say? Why?

TRUST

Q. To what extent is trust present in your workplace? If it is fully present in your working life, congratulations! If there is room for improvement, what role can you play to help build greater levels of trust between you and those who report to you? Between you and your peers and bosses?

PATIENCE

Q. What happens when you are impatient with the people around you? How much does it matter to you? How much do think it should matter? Why?

Q. What would be happening, that is not happening today, if your workplace was more tolerant? What difference would that make?

Q. If your workplace is rife with impatient people at all levels (most are), what part can you play in bringing the impatience quotient down a notch?

ATTITUDE

Q. How does your own attitude help or hinder your ability to lead others through change? What must you be aware of about yourself if you want to bring the "good" kind of attitude to each change project and your workplace?

FAITH

Q. In a time of change, what do you have to believe in before you feel confident in leading others through it?

NOTES

13

FERTILIZING THE CHANGE ENVIRONMENT

 It may be hard for an egg to turn into a bird: it would be a jolly sight harder for it to learn to fly while remaining an egg. We are like eggs at present. And you cannot go on indefinitely being just an ordinary, decent egg. We must be hatched or go bad.

C. S. LEWIS

It's impossible for the human environment to remain the same. Including the workplace. Technology and global demands push you along at a dizzying pace. As a middle leader constantly on the precipice of change, one of your biggest challenges is to create an environment that invites people to break out of their shells and learn to adapt to, and grow with, change.

In this chapter, we'll discuss the three things that must be present for planned change events to be successful. We'll make some important distinctions between caring and care-taking and highlight ways to build enthusiasm and energy among your crew. Finally, we'll talk about the conditions that must be present for people to have the optimal opportunity to accept change, give their best efforts, and work productively.

Focus, Capability, Commitment

The three things that must be present for planned change events to be successful are focus, capability, and commitment.

Focus is about having a clear sense of destination... *what* you want to achieve and *why*; *who* will be involved or affected and; *where* you want to go with it all.

In general, when you're clear with your team about the what, why, who, and where of your planned change, you're in a better position to help them understand and commit to it. Then, you must lock it in. Do this by being consistent with your message and in your daily actions. Also do it by making sure to avoid unnecessary side issues that can distract you. I know. It's not easy to stay on point all of the time. There are so many distractions. But staying focussed on the end goal and the benefits of achieving it will help you and those you lead stay the course.

Commitment is about the attitude, emotion, will, and degree to which there is a sense of ownership in people, enough for them to want a piece of the change being planned.

There was a time when loyalty was key to the staying power of people in organizations. However, today, people who work in companies large and small are not bound or motivated by organizational loyalty. For them to keep going through a difficult change, they have to be engaged in their work and convinced that it is work worth doing. They also need to know what's in it for them, which leads me to the third element of the model... capability.

Capability is about the degree to which skills, knowledge, processes, and resources are present.

To have the focus and vision for a new future is a grand thing. However, without the capability to pull it off, it is only a dream. The development of capability in your organization is key not only to its future success but also to the retention of those who will bring it about. This is where commitment finds its reward. People will commit to staying the course of change if they can learn and grow in the process. The knowledge they gain belongs to them and is something they can take with them wherever they choose to go. This is also true of you. In the meantime, they will likely be more willing to use their enhanced knowledge to bring the organization's planned change from dream to reality. So in the end, everyone wins.

This is all based on a model developed by Hubert Saint-Onge, before his time as founder and principal of Saint-Onge Alliance in Ontario. The model[1] illustrates what must be present for people to make change happen and achieve their goals.

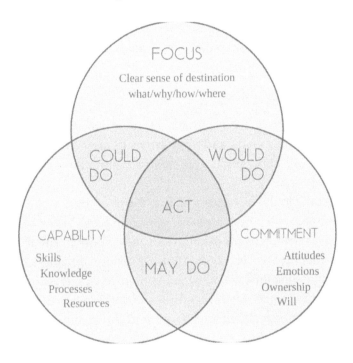

When focus, commitment, and capability come together, you are in the optimal place for *doing* and also for achieving what you set out to do. If any one of the three elements is missing, this is what it might look like:

- Focus and commitment without *capability* makes your change something you *would do* if you had the resources you needed to get it done.
- Commitment and capability without *focus* makes your change something you *may do* if you were clear on *what* it is and *why* you want to go there.

- And capability and focus without *commitment* makes your change something you *could do*, if only you wanted to.
- When focus, capability, and commitment converge, you have all the elements you need to *act* and successfully implement the change.

When preparing to make a change, from your place as a middle leader, give consideration to these three elements because if any are missing, your change initiative could be in jeopardy.

Caring Versus Care-taking

Let's say you've have accomplished a level of focus, commitment, and capability that allows you and your group to move forward with your planned change. How might you care for your team and facilitate its progress?

The word *care* takes on one of two forms: caring and care-taking. Caring provides the best possible opportunity for people to thrive, grow, and contribute. Care-taking does the opposite. The challenge is that like identical twins, each kind of caring, though looking and sounding like the other, is not. Each has a different impact on the workplace and the people who work in it. The difference between caring and care-taking begins with a difference in the assumptions you work from.

Care-taking assumptions:
I know what's best for those who follow me.
If I take care of them, they owe me.
My people are not capable of solving their own problems.
If they do as I ask, I will keep them safe.
As leader, I am also protector.

Caring assumptions:
Those I lead know what's best for them. They like to have choices.

If I care for them, they will care for others including those whom the organization serves.

People I lead are responsible adults.

People are fully capable of solving their own problems.

As leader, I am also facilitator.

For some, the notion of *being taken care of* can actually be appealing, at least at first. In this scenario, when you have a particularly sticky problem, you simply have to take it to your boss and s/he will take it off your hands. As well, decisions that affect you are not usually discussed with you and so if things go wrong you feel quite justified in grumbling about it without having to take responsibility for it. And that can be perversely satisfying.

Eventually, though, even people who initially like the idea of *being taken care of* tire of it and either strain against its limitations and rebel, or retreat, taking their best game with them.

Some believe that creating a caring work environment is akin to laissez-faire leadership[2]. But caring workplaces operate from clearly-stated boundaries communicated through their organizational purpose and a set of values that provide focus and serve as a guide for problem solving and decision-making.

Using those boundaries as a guide, organizations and leaders who care will:

- hold people accountable for the commitments and decisions they make
- provide opportunities for learning and growth
- encourage, coach, and challenge people to build capability
- liberally share problem solving and resist the temptation to "do it themselves"
- acknowledge and reward fine work regularly
- create structures and mechanisms that encourage autonomy and allow for help to be available when it is most needed

Here's the point. Those who care-*take* exercise power over others and operate from the perspective of ownership. Those who *care* are more likely to value collaborative effort and operate from the perspective of shared responsibility.

If you create a caring environment, the likelihood of your gaining commitment from people who work in it will be high. If, however, you choose to exercise your authority over them unnecessarily, even if your motivation is to protect them, you will have difficulty achieving the results you desire.

Unlocking the Energy

> *The Leader's job, after all, is not to provide energy but to release it from others.*

FRANCES HESSELBEIN

I thought that Ms. Hesselbein's remark was an oversimplification of a very difficult job. But then I wondered. What does it actually take for people to unlock hidden reservoirs of energy from others and have them use it willingly in the accomplishment of great work?

Give them something they can relate to and believe in. Work becomes meaningful when people know why it's important and that the part they play in it is equally important. If they can feel that importance, they stop thinking about it as work and start thinking about it as contribution, which is something they do by choice. And that's pretty energizing.

Work with them. I don't mean that you should do the work *they're* doing or be there every minute. No, I mean, *talk* to them from time to time. Let them know they're on the right track. And if they're not, help them to make adjustments. Tell them what they need to do, or be, to succeed. Let them know you're interested in what they're doing. And yes, occasionally, roll up your sleeves and work alongside them. That will help them to build their sense of common purpose. As well, people seem to have more energy when they feel the work they do is important enough for you to pitch in from time to time.

Please don't hover. There is a fine line between working with people and hovering over them[3]. Once they've shown you they know what they're doing, let them get on with it. If you hover, their energy level will plummet. Fast. On the other hand, people can get pretty stoked when they know you trust them to do their part without having to give constant direction.

Give value for contribution. There is nothing more energizing than being acknowledged for a job well done. It doesn't have to be a big deal. However, from time to time, people need to know that what they're doing is appreciated and valued.

And finally, help make work life fun[4]. You don't have to be a constant source of entertainment. There is serious work to be done. But at work, as in life, there are, well, absurdities that just need to be laughed at. People get so much energy from laughter, especially in the company of their colleagues. It breaks any tension that might be hanging around and really helps people to keep a healthy perspective on the tasks ahead.

In my experience, people may be motivated and energized by the promise of material reward, but they are more likely to give their best and push through the hard parts if they feel a sense of belonging and know their work is important and appropriately valued.

And I'll Follow You Anywhere...

As a summary, here is what I would want from you if I were facing a major change and you were my leader.

Paint a picture of the future that includes me. If I can see where I fit and what I might contribute to bringing the picture out of the frame and into reality, I'm in.

Give me direction when I need it and freedom when I've earned it. Sometimes I need you to tell me what to do. But, when I *know* what I'm doing and have all I need to do the work, let me get on with it and I will make you proud.

Help me learn new things and be better than I was before. I want to learn and grow. I have dreams too. Give me what I need to build skill and have experiences that will help me learn. That way, I can be at my best now when you need me, and in the future when you won't.

Ask for my opinion and then really listen when I give it. When I know you are truly interested in what I have to say, I'll spend more time thinking about things that are important to both of us. You don't always have to agree with me. Just listen. Show me that you hear me and understand where I'm coming from.

Expect more from me that I expect from myself. Hey, I'm human. I don't always see what you see when you talk to me or watch me work. And, I'm not always that sure about my own capabilities. If you encourage and challenge me to stretch beyond what *I* think I can do and support me as I give it my best shot, you will have my gratitude.

Trust me first. I know it's tough. I'm going to make mistakes and that's always worrying. But, if I know you're willing to trust me to do my best, I will work toward making you glad you did.

Laugh at yourself and with me. Simply put, if we can make each other laugh from time to time and take ourselves less seriously than the work, I will always enjoy working with you. Really.

Give me the straight goods about how I'm doing. There are going to be times when I need you to tell me something I might not want to hear. Please tell me anyway. If you do, I might be upset at first but will know where I stand. If you don't, it won't go away and more than likely will come back to bite both of us at a most inconvenient time. Put it to me honestly and with good intention and I will receive it with grace.

Live by the rules you set for me. For the most part, I'm okay with rules. Ask me to follow them and I will, if you follow them too. Allow me to challenge them when they are getting in the way of my doing my job. Be open to changing them when necessary. If they can't be changed, help me to understand why. Do that and I will respect and trust you.

Help me to celebrate my successes. Acknowledgement of my accomplishments will always be appreciated. Enough said.

Help me to learn from my failures. When I fail, believe me, I will punish myself enough for both of us. If, instead of punishment or blame, you offer me a chance to examine what went wrong and what I can do better the next time, my failure will have value. I will appreciate that.

Show me your courage and your confidence. There is a certain feeling of reassurance when I see you stand up for your beliefs, values, and the people who follow you, (especially when you stand up for me). When you do that, it makes me proud to be associated with you.

Show me your humanity. I don't expect you to be a super hero. If, from time to time, you show me that you too have doubts and moments of anxiety or fear, I will respect that and do my best to give you my support.

Certainly, for change plans to have a chance to succeed, support mechanisms have to be in place to ensure that people have the best chance of achieving focus, commitment, and capability. As a middle leader, you can create the right environment that allows it to happen. It begins with caring and helping your team find the energy it needs to get through the tough bits. It's a tall order. But it's doable.

THINK ABOUT IT

Before embarking on a change project it might be helpful for you to consider the three elements discussed and contemplate:

FOCUS

Q. Do you fully understand the direction your company is taking with the change?

Q. Do you understand it enough to be able to share it with those who report to you and explain your collective role in it?

Q. Why is this change important?

Q. What will it be like for you when it's done? What could distract you?

Q. How might you avoid such distractions?

Q. How might you achieve even greater clarity?

COMMITMENT

Q. To what extent are you committed to this change?

Q. What do you see as the benefit of making it?

Q. How does it serve your company purpose?

Q. As a middle leader, how does it serve your own purpose and those who report to you?

Q. If you were to paint a picture of the future, after the change has been made, what would be different? How will you fit into that new picture?

Q. What do you need to do to gain commitment for this change from your group, area, or division?

Q. If you're not committed, what do you have to do to get on board...or get out of the way?

CAPABILITY

Q. Do you have the skills you need to do your part? If not, what training do you need and in what format?

Q. Who will you talk to about that? How should you go about getting it?

Q. Do you have the equipment and resources you need? If you do, do you know how to make optimal use of them? If you don't, whom will you talk to about that?

Q. What are the things that will likely get in your way?

Q. How good are you at addressing these things?

CARING OR CARE-TAKING

Q. What assumptions might you be making about the people who report to you?

Q. How correct or useful are those assumptions?

Q. Do you act more as a facilitator or a protector?

Q. How effective are you—in getting things done and building confidence from your chosen perspective?

NOTES

14

GETTING TO ACTION

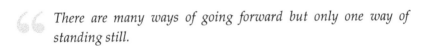 *There are many ways of going forward but only one way of standing still.*

FRANKLIN D. ROOSEVELT

Preparing for change is not the same as actually changing. A lot of organizations are really good at visualizing a new tomorrow and planning strategies for getting there. However, where the rubber meets the road is in the actual doing of the tasks necessary to take them from current state to future one. That's where it tends to get a little fuzzy and messy. Because it's *hard*.

In this chapter we will discuss some of the difficulties you may face as a middle leader when you are in the midst of a planned change: influencing up, delegation (specifically when not to delegate), and the delicate matter of downsizing. We'll also consider the importance of reinforcement of the new way as you go through the change process.

Influencing Up

Generally, influencing others to consider alternate ways of doing something is an intuitive rather than calculated process. Sometimes you become an influencing force simply by being in a room with people. This comes from earning the respect, credibility, and trust we talked about earlier.

At other times you have to be more strategic about it, like when you want to make a change that requires your boss's support and approval. That's a trickier task. After all, you hold no sway over your boss except in your ability to convince them that what you want to do is a good idea that serves an equally good purpose. There may be times when you don't agree with your boss and your intent is to challenge them to rethink their position. That's even trickier.

It requires you to build on your credibility, trust your own ideas, and respect the possibility that your boss may be moved from their position. However, there are four things that will help you increase your potential for influencing upward.

1. KNOW YOUR STUFF. If you are meeting with your boss to convince him to do something he may not have thought about or challenge his thinking, begin by sharing your understanding of the purpose and larger goals of the organization as they relate to the company change plan. That way, you can show the relevance of your ideas and where they fit in the overall scheme of things.

2. APPROACH YOUR MEETING FROM A LEARNING PERSPECTIVE. You may feel strongly about your ideas or concerns but your boss will have a perspective too. If you don't know what it is, do your best to find out. Then you can decide how far apart you are in your views. In that way you will avoid making assumptions and have a more productive discussion.

3. WHEN ASKING QUESTIONS OF YOUR BOSS, KNOW THEY MAY OR MAY NOT HAVE AN IMMEDIATE ANSWER. Questions often trigger deeper thought. Your boss will probably not have all the answers you need, but asking questions will possibly open up conversation and give you an opportunity to resolve issues that are of interest to both of you.

4. IF YOU ARE PRESENTING A NEW IDEA, STRATEGY, OR TACTIC TO YOUR BOSS, BE PREPARED TO OFFER SOMETHING PRACTICAL AND ACTIONABLE TO BEAR IT OUT. If you go to your boss with a new approach to the change plan, or part thereof, ensure you've thought it through and can back it up with something concrete. Otherwise, any influence you may have becomes impotent.

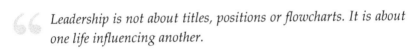

Leadership is not about titles, positions or flowcharts. It is about one life influencing another.

JOHN C. MAXWELL

The Challenge and Responsibility of Delegation

In leadership, one of the things you are always being reminded of is the importance of delegation. With good reason. It ensures an even distribution of work and authority and provides important opportunities for individual exploration and growth, especially in times of change.

However, there are times when, regardless of your leadership position, you have to rely on your strength of character to call upon the backbone and take charge.

Here are some situations where delegation is not an option.

When you have to deliver bad news or make a change that you know will not be well received. Leadership is not about popularity. It involves making hard decisions. Sometimes those decisions affect jobs and the futures of those who do them. It means delivering tough messages personally, staying around to respond to difficult questions, and participating in the process of making hard and sometimes upsetting transitions.

When the objectives of an assignment are unclear or people don't have the tools they need to get the job done. Delegating an assignment that is not well thought out, or does not include the tools necessary for implementation, is to guarantee failure. And it does little for the people charged with carrying it out apart from adding to their frustration level.

Your job as a leader is to ensure clarity around what is to be achieved and to provide the resources necessary to promote success. Turning a concept into an assignment while it is still in its formative stage makes everyone's job harder.

When something goes wrong that affects the entire department or company. Let's say that things are motoring along nicely in your domain. People are attending to their responsibilities and you are delegating assignments in accordance with your knowledge of their capabilities. Great.

And then something goes wrong. Someone makes a big mistake that reverberates beyond your sphere of control, affecting other areas of the organization and its reputation.

While you might have delegated the work assignment, the responsibility for the outcome of it rests with you. That's why you get paid the big bucks. It is your job to find out specifically what went wrong and why. It is your job to work with the person or people involved in bringing the mistake about and taking whatever corrective action is deemed appropriate. And, you are the one that must be accountable to your boss. 'Nuff said.

When you are trying something new and the risk of failure is high. In any change project, innovation is crucial to growth and sustainability. As such, risk is an inherent part of life. If a leader contemplates a project that carries a high risk/reward ratio, it also requires full involvement by the leader. To some extent, this will mitigate the risk and send the message that, while you may be asking others to "go where no man has gone before," you will be right there with them, to share in the glory...or the blame.

The Dreaded Downsizing, Outplacing (a.k.a. Firing), and Those Left Behind

Sometimes leadership is about dismantling something to make room for something else, or reducing something rather than growing it. These are hard times involving difficult conversations, conversations that affect the lives of others...and not always in a good way.

I've been thinking about the times when I've had such conversations with people, when change was afoot, and jobs were diminishing or disappearing altogether. And I've been thinking, too, about how the sting of losing a job can either be eased or made infinitely worse by the person delivering the news. I know this because of Sandra.

Sandra was not performing well. She had been given numerous opportunities to improve, but it became evident that Sandra and her job simply did not fit well together. I was quite new to my role and the prospect of firing someone was unpleasant and scary. I liked Sandra. I also knew she could ill afford to lose her job.

I tried to do it gently. I took her aside and fed her a lot of platitudes to try and smooth away the hurt that was going to come. I talked and talked. I 'ummed' and 'aahed.' I skirted and danced and took care of my own discomfort first. When our interview ended, I was sure that I had delivered the message well. At least *I* felt better.

In fact, I was quite pleased with myself, even a little smug. Until the next day... when Sandra came to work as usual having no idea she had been fired the day before.

Of course I had to do it again. And this time, I had to cut to the chase. It was embarrassing for both of us. It was doubly distressing for Sandra because her embarrassment was heaped on top of the shock of realizing that she no longer had a job. She didn't deserve that.

If I had been braver and more direct I might have spared her dignity. As it was, I know she blamed herself for not getting the message even though it was entirely my fault. It was a bad job on my part and I have never forgotten the lesson I took from it.

Middle leaders are often called upon to deliver the kind of bad news I had to give to Sandra. Let's pretend now that you are my boss and you have to tell me that I no longer have a job. I'm fired. It's a nerve-wracking proposition, I know, and one that you'd probably give anything to be able to delegate. But you can't. So it's you and me, kid. And, when the time comes, here's what I'm going to need from you.

The straight goods. Beating about the bush might make you feel better, but it won't help me. Come to the point right away. Do not launch into a soliloquy about the company's challenges, concerns, or plans before letting me have it. After all, I'm not going to be part of your future. And really, at this point, I'm not likely to care, am I? Simply tell me you have bad news and then tell me what it is. If I want an explanation after that (and I most likely will), I'll ask for it.

Some direction. Before we sit down together, please be prepared to tell me what is to happen immediately after our interview and in the ensuing period. I will feel a little stunned and disoriented. If you antici-pate this and make sure that all the information and documentation I need to begin the process of moving on is promptly available to me, it will help me feel just a little safer.

Some support. I may not need or want you to "hold my hand," but it's possible that I will need you to listen to me. This may take time. Please allow me this. If I am emotional, give me a tissue, and the benefit of your quiet presence. If I am angry, allow me to vent just a little. I may say things I don't mean. To use the vernacular, suck it up. It's not about you.

Your professionalism. I know delivering this kind of news is hard. For this reason you might be tempted to say things that will sound, well, empty and insincere. I need you to practice what you are going to say to me so that when the time comes, you'll deliver your message with clar-ity, empathy, and without apology. There's a difference between feeling sorry and apologizing. Don't get the two mixed up.

My dignity intact. Please allow me to make a dignified exit from the workplace. I am not a criminal. My job may be redundant but *I'm* not. Please do not frog march me out of the premises with my potted plant and my personal items in a box or demand my keys and passwords in front of my peers. The truth is, I'm more likely to speak well of you and the company if you treat me with respect.

Here's the bottom line on this. Terminating someone's employment is one of the most difficult things a leader must do. It is important to remember, though, that it is *infinitely more difficult for the person on the receiving end.* Doing all you can to help that person make a dignified and minimally-painful transition to their next step is simply the right thing to do.

Remember Those Left Behind

During times of change, when there is a lot of movement, and jobs become redundant, the initial emphasis is on the people who are leaving. This is understandable. However, if you're wise, you will remember the impact that watching their colleagues leaving will have on those who remain. There's some work to do here as well.

First, you have to tell the survivors the bad news. They will be concerned for their colleagues. And they'll be wondering whether there is still a queue to the chopping block and whether they're in it.

People who are worried about their own jobs will not be able to focus on helping you or your company move into the future. So, tell them as much as you can about what has taken place, keeping in mind the need to protect the confidentiality and dignity of those on the way out. People who are staying will want to know that those who are leaving will be okay. If you can assure them that you and the company have played your part in that, chances are, you will all be able to move on.

Then, focus on the future.

The quicker you can point people in a future direction, the less time they will have to mourn the past. Be prepared to repeat your company's new vision and goals. Explain how your area of responsibility and the people who work in it have an important role to play. Then, give them something to do. Give them work that is aligned with the new direction of the company. Challenge and encourage them. Acknowledge short-term results ensuring to connect these achievements to the future vision and goals.

Those who survive a company re-organization also need to know that they too will be okay. Keeping them informed about what's going on will help them process what has happened and move forward with greater confidence and enthusiasm for what is ahead.

Reinforcing the New

Let's now assume that you and everyone who works with you have come to appreciate the need and urgency for change. You have all signed on and things are underway. What's next? Reinforcement.

For analogy, I'm drawn to the time I stopped smoking. I had been thinking of quitting for a while, not for any noble reason, but because my office building was about to be declared a smoke-free zone and I didn't fancy smoking on the street. Also because I was told that smoking would give me wrinkles. (I am nothing if not vain.)

In spite of my initial enthusiasm, as I moved through the process of changing from a smoker to a non-smoker, my commitment to it began to wane. The new vision I held of myself as a non-smoker started to blur and the temptation to revert to my old ways grew stronger. That's pretty typical, even when we *choose* to change. That's why reinforcement is vital.

Here is how you, as a middle leader involved in a major change project, can provide reinforcement.

Watch and listen. Over the course of the change process, people will suffer in a variety of ways. When I stopped smoking, I gained weight. I contracted shingles. And I experienced inexplicable emotional melt-downs. While this may not be a consequence of organizational change, you can bet there will be other kinds of suffering and stress in the air. Watching carefully and listening for the signs will allow you the opportunity to anticipate the negative effects of change and mitigate them to avoid the potential for derailment.

Keep the empathy coming. I believe people are more willing to stay the course of change when their leaders genuinely strive to understand and share their feelings during each stage of the process. That means travelling down the road with them and bringing your own emotions with you.

Keep everyone's eyes on the prize. Just as I had to be reminded and continually imagine life as a non-smoker, as a leader of a change initiative you must keep the new vision alive in the hearts and minds of people who follow you. I needed someone to tell me that my suffering would, in the end, be worthwhile. So will they.

Burn the bridges that lead back to the old world. If you want people to move away from the old world, you have to render that world unattainable. For example, I was no longer going to be able to enjoy smoking at my desk or even in the cafeteria at work. That world was gone. And so, even if I wanted to go back to the way things were, I couldn't. No pun intended but the bridge had been burned. So, ask yourself: to what extent have I dismantled the trappings of our old world?

Model what you want to see. No matter how much encouragement my colleagues who smoked gave me in my quest to stop, it was hard for me to believe them as they offered me their best advice between cigarette breaks. Being mindful of your own actions as you move through change keeps things real for everyone. If you want others to change, you have to change too. And you have to go first.

Recognize and acknowledge behaviour and actions that align with the new. Real change comes about when you begin to notice new behaviour and actions in others. When this happens, acknowledge those who are consciously and unconsciously bringing the change to fruition. It is a prime opportunity for reinforcement, especially for those people who continue to struggle with the prospect of embracing the new world.

No matter how well-planned or thought-out, when you start putting your plans into action, change initiatives always get messy. While you may not, as a middle leader, be part of the initial planning and high-level strategizing, you and your peers will be in the thick of it when it gets to the execution part.

To participate fully and be counted, there will be times when you will have to call upon your powers of influence to be heard, to present ideas that may not have been considered, and to challenge those who are more senior to you in service of a better result.

There will be times when, as much as you want to, you cannot delegate difficult work to others. These include times when change means reducing jobs and displacing people who do them. And when that's done, there will be times when the ongoing, sometimes even tedious, work of reinforcement, will be vitally necessary to ensure you all come out the other side of change in a better place than you were before.

That means wherever you go, your courage will have to go with you. I think too that in times of change there is great opportunity to push out from the middle, expand your sphere of influence and make a positive difference in your own life and the lives of those around you. In all the messiness of change, that can be extremely satisfying.

THINK ABOUT IT

Q. How much upward and lateral influence do you believe you currently have? For example, do your peers and bosses:

- hang on your every word?
- consider your opinion, accept your ideas as valid and act on some of them?
- consider your opinion; disagree but give you credit for trying?
- give lip service to your opinion but dismiss it, in a diplomatic way, as having no value?
- not let you through the door?

Q. Considering your responses to question one, what might you do to build on your current ability to influence others, participate in the direction your company is going and the decisions it makes?

Q. As a middle leader, what do you refuse to delegate? Why? How does not delegating these things serve those who report to you? Or serve your organization?

Q. When there are changes that eliminate jobs in your organization, how much attention do you typically pay to those who "survive" a downsizing? To what extent do you think this is important? Why?

Q. How do you help your staff concentrate on the future when all around you seems to be "up in the air"? How do you do it for yourself? What might you need more of or less of? From your place in the middle, what can you do to help get what you need?

NOTES

15

BUILDING STRENGTH THROUGH STRUGGLE

 My barn having burned down, I can now see the moon.

MIZUTA MASAHIDE, SEVENTEENTH CENTURY JAPANESE
POET AND SAMURAI

Change, be it planned or unplanned, is an inevitable consequence of being alive. You feel its impact every day at work and at home. Maybe you wonder what you might possibly gain from the barrage of things new, different, revolutionary, or otherwise disruptive in your daily life.

There is one valuable thing we all gain from having lived through change time and again. It's called resilience: that ability to recover quickly from change events, discover stores of inner strength we didn't know we had, move forward with greater confidence and a kind of wisdom that only comes from having lived.

In this chapter, we will talk about what it takes to build resilience. We will look at the value of using that strength to challenge the status quo. And, we'll also talk about why, on its own, toughing it out during times of change is not always enough to ensure a successful outcome.

Resilience is not exclusively reserved for human beings. You could say it makes the world go round. Witness the snowdrops that grow up through hard, cold ground every spring to remind us of balmy days to come. Consider the trees and bushes, seeming quite dead during winter's harshness, bursting forth with new buds and leaves as soon as the first warm day rides in on a mild breeze. Resilience, that ability to bend, stretch, change, and grow strong is how all living things survive and ultimately thrive.

The Hermit Crab

On a Caribbean island off the coast of Belize lives the hermit crab. Hermit crabs use abandoned shells to protect their softer, more vulnerable parts. These shells represent portable homes and are key to the hermit crab's survival. However, as the crab grows, so does its need for larger accommodations. When it's time to change shells, he'll make for the beach in search of the perfect one.

When a new shell appears on the shore, a collection of hermit crabs gathers to try it out. They arrange themselves in a line, from largest to smallest, with a view to exchanging homes with each other. If the new shell is too large for any one of them, they wait for the right-sized crab to come along and claim the new shell so the exchange can begin.

I saw this process on an episode of BBC Earth and was fascinated by the orderly manner in which the crabs moved out of their old homes and into new ones. Of course it didn't always go perfectly well. What change effort does?

At some point in the exchange, a new hermit crab arrived, not having been part of the original queue. He pushed his way into the line and took a shell away from a smaller crab, leaving the little one scrambling to find alternate housing. There was a bit of a panic for a while but the little crab finally found a shell to cover him adequately until the next exchange. He would survive this round but only in the knowledge that his new home was not quite what he was looking for. It had a hole in it.

In any episode of change, (or *ex*-change in the case of the little crab), you won't always come out the other side with exactly what you expect. There will sometimes be disappointment. There will sometimes be surprise. There will sometimes be unimagined success. And there will sometimes be failure. Whatever the outcome, with each experience, what you can count on is that the struggle means you're developing another layer of resilience that will make you stronger and help you move on to the next thing with greater confidence.

Breaking Rules ... a.k.a. Daring to Put Cat Among Pigeons

If resilience gives you the strength to adapt and move on, let's look at how it also might give you the confidence to challenge the status quo, specifically when it comes to rules.

In general, rules are put in place to ensure personal safety and to keep things in balance. They are also imposed in organizational settings to provide structure that support the work and to build a broad framework within which individuals are free to operate and contribute.

Some people are of the opinion that rules are made to be broken. In fact, they are so convinced of this, they see no point in learning them in the first place. The resulting behaviour from this laissez-faire approach is a kind of chaos that serves no one in the end. It lacks maturity and, I hazard to say, increases rather than diminishes the need for more rules.

But sometimes rules really do only serve to get in the way.

In a world where the ability to improvise is key to success, yester-day's rules can be today's impediment. Old rules often slow the flow of progress, sometimes down to a trickle. They stifle creativity and innova-tion. And they create roadblocks to the implementation of needed change. From this perspective, I think it safe to say that the work of lead-ership includes breaking rules.

From your particular middle leadership position, you may not consider it your place to break rules or change them. However, it is likely that you and those who follow you are the ones who find yourselves having to work with them the most. And if certain rules are getting in the way of your ability to lead your area of responsibility through change, perhaps it's time for you to challenge them. Or even dare to break them.

However, before you go off and begin declaring war on rules, I think you need some, um, rules, to ensure that the breaking process provides as great an opportunity for a positive result as possible. Here are two such rules that work for me.

1. *Before eliminating or dismissing existing rules, seek to understand why they were made in the first place.* It's easy to make assumptions about why rules were made. But before completely ignoring them, it's wise to question their initial purpose. If that purpose proves to be no longer relevant, then throwing them out is probably a good thing.
2. *Be prepared to accept the consequences that may come from circumventing or defying rules.* There is always the chance that circumventing a rule can cause grief for someone else somewhere else—in the organization or outside it. Breaking an established rule comes with a measure of risk. As they often say in retail stores about handling merchandise, "If you break it you buy it." Owning your choice to break rules in service of facilitating change is part of being a responsible leader.

Having said all of that, I confess I'm an inveterate rule follower. I, like other baby boomers, was generally raised to follow and respect the rules. And yet, in my growing (ahem) maturity, I see the need to continually question those rules that make no sense to me. After all, rules are conceived and administered by people. And most rules will come to a place where they are no longer useful or relevant to our lives or businesses.

If you are to encourage innovation and change, you must also accept that rules should be subject to rigorous scrutiny to determine their appropriateness in changing times. Settling for something because *that's the rule* or *that's the way it is* will get in the way of your progress. Helping others adapt quickly to new and changing circumstances may well require you to have the courage to break a few rules along the way.

Lessons from The Old Man and the Sea

When it comes time to change something major in your work or home life, resilience and courage are your friends. However, on their own, they will not ensure a successful outcome. For that you need something more.

While channel surfing one day, I caught a glimpse of Spencer Tracy playing Santiago in *The Old Man and the Sea*. It didn't register much at the time because, as you may know, when one channel surfs, the little grey cells take a nap. Later though, I began to think about the story and the lessons it has to teach.

For those who are unfamiliar with the story, Santiago is an old fisherman living in a village not far from Havana. Fishing is his livelihood and yet he has failed to catch any fish in eighty-four days. The father of the young boy who usually goes out with Santiago has instructed the boy to stay away from the old man. He is *bad luck*. So Santiago goes fishing alone.

On the eighty-fifth day, he decides to go out farther than he usually does because somewhere within him, he believes there is a big fish just meant for him. His instinct proves to be correct as his hook and bait are swallowed by a marlin so large it dwarfs the boat.

The old man is determined to catch this fish. He wants to prove that he isn't bad luck. He envisions bringing the giant fish into the tiny harbour of his home with enough to feed the whole village. Perhaps, deep down, he likes the idea of being a hero.

So, Santiago hangs onto the fishing line with all his might. The fish fights valiantly all the while dragging the boat farther and farther out to sea. The old man suffers as the line cuts through the muscle of his hands and his back goes into spasms of pain from pulling and resisting.

In the end, the fish tires enough to allow the old man to reel him in closer to the boat. It is then that Santiago is successful in sinking his harpoon into the fish's heart. The battle is won but the war is just beginning. The old man realizes the fish is bigger than the boat. So with great diligence and respect, he straps the fish to the side of the boat and begins the very long journey home.

The marlin is ravaged again and again by sharks. And, as much as the old man fights to preserve it, he fails. By the time he reaches home, he is completely exhausted... and the fish is reduced to a skeleton.

Santiago's ability to stay the course and fight for his dream of bringing in a big fish, even in the most unfavourable of conditions, is something to be admired. The trouble is, in the end, he had nothing to show for this tenacity. It could be that he believed his skill as a fisherman and his determination to stay the course and prove himself to others was enough. He believed he just had to keep going and if he was tough enough and stuck it out, he would win in the end.

Santiago made a bold move. He clung to the belief (that the big fish was out there) and the dream (of redemption when he returned to his village a hero), but lacked a plan. Dreams do not come to fruition without having a plan, some kind of structure that will give you the best chance for making a successful change.

As a middle leader you will be part of the planning process when your organization instigates change. After all, the wing-and-prayer method used by Santiago is not the practice of choice in most successful workplaces.

There are two things Santiago and many workplaces spend too little time on.

1. Think Beyond the Achievement of the Goal

To consider achievement of the goal as the end would be a mistake. You also have to anticipate what might happen next, especially in the event of a huge success. What then? How will you manage it? What more will you need? How will it change you? How might it change those you lead or other people in your life?

Perhaps if Santiago had thought beyond catching the big fish and included the resources he needed or relationships he had to build to ensure he could bring it home intact, his story would have ended differently.

In our own lives, the same holds true. For instance, let's look at Mary's goal of losing 100 pounds to help her manage her diabetes and myriad other health issues. There are complex issues that arise from losing weight, like being attractive for perhaps the first time ever or being noticed everywhere she goes. If Mary doesn't think about that, doesn't try to get help and support for how she is going to respond to that new level of attention, she may unwittingly scupper her weight-loss success, regain weight, and return to the safer invisibility of obesity.

2. Know When to Cut the Line

Where is your point of no return? In the case of Santiago, going farther and farther out to sea ensured that by the time he made it back to shore, there would be nothing left of the fish. The gain was not worth the pain. In business and in life, we also have to know when to stop, change, or let go. Doing so in a timely way, although not terribly pleasant, ensures that we can take our lumps, learn from them, and move on more quickly.

Striking out to explore new territory is an essential part of leadership. However, the success of such exploration and the achievement of goals rely on one's ability to marry leadership skill with management ability.

As well, you might agree that Santiago lacked neither toughness nor courage. But being tough and brave doesn't always build resilience. The measure of his resilience will come not only from this, but also from his willingness to adapt his perspectives based on what he learned, change his approach, and try again with a better outcome firmly in mind. The same holds true for the rest of us.

Building an inner core of strength comes through struggle. It is the reward we earn for having experienced and lived through change. The more resilient we become, the more equipped we are to fully participate, challenge rules that maintain the status quo and see change, not as something to fear, but something that is an inevitable part of life.

THINK ABOUT IT

RESILIENCE

Q. What is it in your life that hasn't killed you but made you stronger? If this thing that made you stronger hadn't happened, what would you not know that you know now because it did?

RULES

Company rules are a necessary part of organizational life, however in your role as a middle leader, there are times when rules get in the way of progress.

Q. When was the last time a rule got in the way of your progress, or the progress of a project you were leading?

Q. Was there a time when you did not challenge an existing rule even though it was getting in the way? What was the result?

Q. If you broke a longstanding company rule, what did you learn? What were the consequences if any?

Q. If you haven't, but are thinking about rules in your organization that don't seem to work any more, what might you do to call attention to them?

Q. With whom would you consult before making a move to challenge, discontinue, or propose changes to a rule?

FUTURE CHANGE

Q. So, if the only thing you can count on is change, what do you see as your next one?

Q. To what extent have you thought beyond the accomplishment of this change?

Q. How will you meet the needs of your new environment and the possibilities it could hold for you?

Q. In thinking about your next change, what might be your point of no return?

Q. How will you know when you are approaching the point of no return? In other words, if your change is not having the desired results, at what point might you have to re-evaluate and try something else?

NOTES

NOW'S THE TIME

In a way, it's hard to separate leadership from personhood. It could be said that every time we make a decision to do something different from established practice or routine, we're leading ourselves away from one thing and toward another. Maybe that's why we refer to it as *leading our lives*. But however you look at it, leadership, or the opportunity for it, is present in each of us whether we have invited it or not. Of course it requires some recognition, some development, and some intestinal fortitude to bring it out in all its glory and messiness. But it's there. So if you are in charge of the work of others, know you have it in you to lead those others through whatever changes you will face together.

The pages of this book have offered stories, ideas, and tools for thinking and moving toward purposeful leadership. It begins with choosing something different and then taking a leap of faith that your choice is the right one. In truth, while there is a section dedicated to the subject of change, really, this entire book is about change, change in both thinking and doing. If your efforts are not always met with success, it is no matter. You will live to choose another way on another day, firmly holding lessons learned in your personal arsenal of things tried. After all, mistakes and failures are all part of it but they serve a useful purpose when considering what comes next.

I've been thinking, too, that being in the middle is not a bad thing. It's just a thing. And as I alluded to earlier, it's also just the middle, not the end.

Your Perspective Differs

You have something the less experienced in your organization do not. That is, a wider perspective of life and perhaps a deeper understanding that things don't always work out as planned. In leadership, this understanding is helpful because if Warren Bennis is correct in describing leadership as more jazz than symphony, you are well equipped to improvise when the need arises. You need only to get a fix on why your part of the company exists, whom it is there to serve, and how it connects to the larger organization. With this wider view and from your position in the middle, you can open doors to the greater possibility of using your influence to achieve more than just your business targets. Know that your role as a leader in the middle is about much more than that. It is about working for a purpose. And it's also about making more leaders.

Let's think about that for a minute in the context of your role as a middle leader.

ckWhen you choose leadership on purpose, what is the impact on you and on others? How might things be different from your current experience? What would making more leaders do for your working life or for the world outside it for that matter? These are all questions that require some thought, I know. I also know that somewhere inside you there are answers. And I know too, that you will find them.

For me, it began as a fleeting thought when I was in my late thirties. You know, the kind of thought that swoops in like a baby hummingbird, hovers for a second, and then flies swiftly away again. But it was just enough to tip it over into idea territory. It went like this:

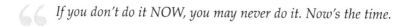 *If you don't do it NOW, you may never do it. Now's the time.*

You may have had a version of that thought. If so, *In the Thick of It* will have helped you move your own wisp of an idea into some actionable thinking, not just as a leader but also as a person, in the middle or otherwise. From where you are, in the thick of it, challenge yourself. Question old mindsets and try new things.

Because now's the time.

And you are ready.

IF YOU LIKED "IN THE THICK OF IT"

*If you enjoyed **In the Thick of It**, please consider leaving a brief review on the website or with the retailer where you bought the book.*

Reviews are is very important to every author. Your feedback doesn't have to be long or detailed. Just a sentence saying what you enjoyed.

Please accept my thanks if this is something you'd like to do.

ACKNOWLEDGMENTS

If, ten years ago, I had even a fleeting thought about writing a book, I would have dismissed it as an impossible dream. Where would I begin? What would make me think I could even write coherently or offer anything from which anyone could gain useful insight? Okay, that last part has still yet to be proven. But I'm feeling pretty confident at the moment that *In the Thick of It* has something to offer you if only to make you stop and think about your own life and your role in the middle of it all. I have people to thank for that.

It was the blog that began it all. Well, actually there were two blogs. The first one was entitled, "Miss Prissy Perfection" and contained random stories and thoughts that came to mind on any particular day. Miss Prissy is one of my inner critics. I don't have much to thank her for.

However, it was my son **Rob Jones** who encouraged me to start it and also to join Twitter, bringing me further into the twenty-first century and to the world of social media. Truthfully, I'm not sure whether to thank Rob or blame him for that. Social media can be a curse as well as a blessing. However in the end, the second blog, the one about people and leadership called "You're Not the Boss of Me" turned out to be surprisingly well received. I'm grateful for that and for Rob's encouragement.

I'm grateful too, to all the people who read it, found it useful, and recommended it to others. Thank you.

Somewhere along the line, a few people started asking, "So when are you going to write a book?"

It was an intriguing thought. But as mentioned, I didn't know. And I didn't know how. Enter **Boni and John Wagner Stafford of Ingenium Books** who have guided, coached, and cajoled me through the process of book writing. Without them, this book would still be among the wool of my imagination and the vision and focus for it unclear. Thank you Boni and John.

Thank you too to **Stephen and Virginia Teatro** who introduced me to Ingenium Books and the possibilities it held for me as an author. I'm grateful that you saw potential in the blog that perhaps I didn't fully appreciate.

My friend, **Maureen Hannah,** was one of the people who helped me learn and shape my views about leadership. She was once my teacher and later, on occasion, she would ask me to work with her in developing a leadership course that she later delivered to students at Vancouver Community College and other public and private organizations. Some of the ideas we came up with together are included in this book. Thank you, Maureen. We've always made a pretty good team.

Recently, I watched my son **Peter Jones** make and carry out some pretty big decisions in his life. Peter didn't know exactly what he wanted but he knew it was time for a change. And he knew what he *didn't* want. For him, that was enough. So he, with his wife Nadine, packed up all their worldly goods and moved from Vancouver back to Ontario to live in the town where he was born.

For quite a while, the road to his new normal was rocky, filled with uncertainty and disappointment. However, he kept going, eventually finding his new place in the world and feeling much better for having made the effort.

Peter's story is not unusual, as in middle age, he has come to that place of internal inquiry, the one that asks us to think about what's next. His story has confirmed, for me at least, the relevance of *In the Thick of It* for others who also find themselves in the middle, between the last thing and the next thing.

As mentioned, not everyone who reads this will be a designated leader but most certainly will be taking the lead in his or her own life and having an impact on those around them as it unfolds. To watch Peter and Nadine go through the process of change was worrying, but also inspiring. Thanks, Pete, for allowing me to be an observer in your life and also perhaps a little voice in your ear from time to time.

I think too, that this is a good place to thank and acknowledge my big sister, **Diane Reynolds.** Diane and I haven't lived in the same province for over thirty years. Our lives are, and have been, very different. And yet, no matter what is going on in my life, she is always there to either help me celebrate or commiserate when times get tough. From the beginning of writing this book, she has been in my corner cheering me on, as she has been all my life. I'd like to think that I do the same for her but I'm not sure that's true. Thank you, Diane, for all you do and all you are.

It's hard to decide what to say about the love and support my husband **Don Teatro** has given me, not just over the course of writing this book but from the very beginning of our life together, twenty-five years ago. He has always believed in me even when I didn't believe in myself. I don't know what I did to deserve him but I will always be grateful. Thank you, Don…for everything.

Finally, this would be an incomplete list of acknowledgements if I failed to mention those who, on hearing I was writing a book, helped keep me going through the writing process with their enthusiasm and unwavering encouragement. It has all meant so much to me. If you're wondering if this part of my expression of gratitude includes you, it does. Really. Thank you.

ABOUT THE AUTHOR

Gwyn Teatro started her career in the mailroom of a large financial institution in Toronto, Ontario. At the tender age of eighteen, her education as a student of human nature was to begin there, as she sat between two middle-aged Scottish veterans, Dave McNeillie and Eddie Killen. There she opened letters and listened to their opinions about the leadership skills of various managers to whom they delivered mail. Dave and Eddie also taught her more than she needed to know about "the language profane." But, over the ensuing years, even that has had its useful moments.

Today, Gwyn is a Certified Professional Coach with a Master of Science degree in management. She has spent the bulk of her career as an HR professional in the financial services industry where she coached senior business leaders and groups on leadership, organizational effectiveness, and strategic business planning. Active on social media and an award-winning blogger on HR and leadership trends and issues, Gwyn has learned a lot about building, that is, building relationships, building bridges, building alliances, and building credibility.

Author photo credit: Tamea Byrd Photography

READING REFERENCES

I know that nonfiction works sometimes call for an annotated bibliography meant to substantiate and lend credibility to the substance of the book. But as this book is not an academic journal, I have instead opted to provide a list of books that have influenced my thinking, observations, experiences, and actions. This seems to me the best way to give credence to much of the content you've read here. Also, if I'm honest, it gives me the best opportunity to minimize the minutia associated with the more detailed accounting, something that would surely contribute to my disappearing up my own backside, an adventure I'd prefer not to experience.

The books mentioned are listed alphabetically by author. Some of them are admittedly dry as dust but nonetheless have managed, somewhere in their contents, to implant an idea in my head that I considered gold. A culmination of both reading about and experiencing many of the concepts found in these books has served to fuel the perspective I hold about leadership and share in my own book.

Adams, John D. *Transforming Leadership, From Vision to Results* (Miles River Press, 1009 Duke Street, Alexandria, Virginia, 1986)

Transforming Leadership covers a lot of ground. There are many contributing authors each providing insight into what it is that makes a transformational leader. It was written and compiled in the late 1980s when command and control leadership was the stick of choice. It served to challenge that notion with something more empowering. And its content is as relevant today as ever.

Here, I learned about the transforming power of working to a shared purpose and having a vision that transcends individual agendas. This is where purpose dictates actions and the commitments we make. It occurred to me while studying from this textbook how very necessary it is, especially now, to lead from the perspective that human beings are not helpless, in fact are fully capable of making a positive difference just by thinking differently and acting from that different platform.

Blanchard, Ken and Jesse Lyn Stoner. *Full Steam Ahead! Unleash the Power of Vision in Your Work and Your Life* (Berrett-Koehler Publishers, Inc., San Francisco, 2011)

This book is about the importance of developing a clear vision for the future, especially in times of change. Let's face it, in the twenty-first century when are we *not* changing? Having an idea about where you're going and being able to articulate a purpose for going there actually helps relieve the anxiety associated with moving through change. Blanchard and Stoner do a great job of taking the reader through the process of change from vision to reality in an uncomplicated and helpful way.

Block, Peter. *The Empowered Manager: Positive political Skills at Work* (Jossey-Bass Publishers, San Francisco, 1991)

This book was written for middle managers and focusses on the value of making meaning and purpose a greater priority over position and rank. It also emphasizes the importance of self-awareness, vision, autonomy and service to others. For me, its main message is that empowerment starts with self. Once we recognize our own power, it is less difficult to empower others. This may sound ethereal but bureaucracy and bad politics are really enemies of productivity. Empowerment is key to achieving optimal results and maintaining an engaged workforce.

Briggs Myers, Isabel, and Peter B. Myers. *Gifts Differing, Understanding Personality Type* (Davies-Black Publishing, Palo Alto, CA, 1980)

It is no secret that I am a particular fan of the Myers Briggs Personality Type Indicator. I like it because somehow it manages to describe the sixteen personality types so accurately it makes self-identification quite easy for most people. Understanding personality type is extremely useful in predicting group conduct. It allows for a measure of tolerance between and among people of diverse outlooks and behaviour. And that is always a good thing. It also points out that even people with similar values can perceive and learn things differently. Understanding this is an invaluable tool for any leader in the middle.

Drucker, Peter F. *Managing in a Time of Great Change* (Harvard Business School Publishing Corp, 2009)

I think it might have been Peter Drucker who first came up with the term "knowledge worker." He was a visionary, able (it seemed) to predict change in society and technology, and by association change in the workplace long before anyone else. Drucker saw the worth in workplaces that value alliances, collaboration, and shared responsibility. In this book, he writes about the changing role of the manager from one whose focus is command and control to one who achieves better results through coaching. He also champions change and the notion that uncertainty was to become a regular visitor to the workplace.

Gallagher, BJ, and Warren H. Schmidt. *A Peacock in the Land of Penguins* (Berrett Koehler Publishers, Inc., Oakland, CA, Fourth Edition 2015)

I think I must have read the first edition of this book as it was quite some time ago. It made a deep impression on me as a reader and also in the way I looked at the people around me. In my rather traditional organization, there was a lot of talk about introducing fresh ideas into our workplace and so from time to time we hired people who where considered "different." It was meant to shake us up a bit and help us look at things in new ways, but instead it seemed we spent our time doing our level best to make them "conform." This book clearly illustrates how this happens and helps us understand the value in embracing difference as well as the pointlessness of engaging people with different talents only to force them into a box that is clearly not for them.

Goleman, Daniel, Richard Boyatzis, and Annie,McKee. *Primal Leadership, Unleashing the Power of Emotional Intelligence* (Harvard Business Review Press, 2013)

This book points out that the best organizations create resonant rather than dissonant working environments. It asserts that emotions are contagious and people depend on each other for emotional cues and stimuli. This is true regardless of your place in an organization. The goal is to develop competencies that align with the creation of resonance because a resonant workplace is one that includes empathy, trust, and a focus on service, all of which tends to get you more of the results you want without the angst associated with a discordant atmosphere.

Johnson, Spencer. *Who Moved My Cheese?* (G.P. Putnam's Sons, a member of Penguin Putnam Inc, New York, NY, 1998)

Who doesn't like a good parable? *Who Moved My Cheese?* became wildly popular in the late '90s. To me, it took something that could be complicated and made it quite simple. The lesson I took from it is, when it comes to change, no matter how much we struggle to keep things the way they've always been, in the end, that struggle becomes fruitless. Either we take measures to anticipate change and seek out "new cheese" or we wait until forced to do something differently in order to survive. Getting ahead of that curve wherever possible just makes sense.

Pink, Daniel. *Drive: The Surprising Truth About What Motivates Us.* (Rivershead Books, An imprint of Penguin, Random House L.L.C, New York, NY., 2009)

Daniel Pink offers some evidence that monetary rewards for good performance and the traditional "carrot and stick" method of motivating people to do their best actually doesn't work. Ironically, his research showed that the larger the reward, the poorer the performance. It also revealed that as human beings, to perform at our best we need three things: autonomy, mastery, and purpose. As a human being myself, I have always thought this made great sense. That's why I mention it in Chapter 10 of this book.

Quinn, Robert E., Sue R. Faerman, Michael P. Thompson, and Michael R. McGrath. *Becoming a Master Manager, A Competency Framework* (Wiley, Hoboken, NJ, 2002)

This book highlighted for me the complexities involved in the role of "Manager." In truth managers assume many roles, whether managing at work or at home. Those roles include director, producer, coordinator, monitor, mentor, facilitator, innovator, and broker. The key to all of these, at least for me, is in knowing when to do what. And that takes leadership.

Schein, Edgar H. *Process Consultation; Lessons for Managers and Consultants* (Addison-Wesley Publishing Company, Reading, Mass. 1987)

Here Edgar Schein offers the O.R.J.I. model I mentioned in Section II: Communication. I came across it in my earlier studies and to be honest have forgotten most of its other content. However, this particular nugget stayed with me because the number of times I have jumped to intervention before taking the time to first find out what was really going on cannot be counted. I rather suspect I'm not unique in this.

Senge, Peter M. *The Fifth Discipline: The Art & Practice of The Learning Organization* (Doubleday / Currency, 666 Fifth Ave, New York NY, 2006)

This book showed me how personal mastery, mental models, team learning, shared vision, and systems thinking all contribute to an organization's ability to move and grow with the times, and how to do so in a functional way. For me, there is a significant message for the individual here. The message is that whatever we choose to do, our actions will have an impact somewhere else in the system. Kind of like a drop of water in a still pond, there will be ripples expanding from the centre of each action that touch the lives and work of others. That's why in this book I talk about checking the impact our words, actions, and even our body language are having on those around us.

Whitworth, Laura, Henry Kimsey-House, and Phil Sandahl. *Co-Active Coaching: New Skills for Coaching People toward Success in Work and Life* (Davies-Black Publishing, Palo Alto, California 1998)

I came across Whitworth, Kimsey-House and Sandahl's book while training for my own coaching certification. There are numerous learning points here about coaching. However, one of the most important ones is this: *It is not the job of a coach to fix people.* This book asserts that a successful coaching relationship begins with the perspective that people are naturally creative, resourceful, and whole. Also, a good coach cannot separate one area of a person's life from the rest. A whole life is essentially a whole system. One part of it is bound to affect another.

Whitmore, John. *Coaching for Performance; the New Edition of the Practical Guide* (Nicholas Brealey Publishing, London, 2000)

Whitmore offers another useful model when coaching for results. The GROW model has been around for a while. It is more formulaic in nature and is a good problem-solving tool as well. It asks us to determine **Goals, Reality, Options** and the four **W**'s: **What** (is to be done?) **Why** (should I do it?) **When** (must it be done?) and by **Whom?**

This is a good instructional book for any middle leader who wants to practice their coaching skills.

NOTES

2. Changing the Narrative

1. http://en.wikipedia.org/wiki/James_C._Collins
2. http://en.wikipedia.org/wiki/Adolf_Hitler
3. http://en.wikipedia.org/wiki/Jim_Jones
4. http://en.wikipedia.org/wiki/Osama_bin_Laden
5. http://en.wikipedia.org/wiki/Transformational_leadership

5. Transmission

1. https://en.wikipedia.org/wiki/johari_window

13. Fertilizing the Change Environment

1. http://www.banffexeclead.com/onge.html
2. http://psychology.about.com/od/leadership/f/laissez-faire-leadership.htm
3. http://www.ncmahq.org/files/Articles/ECB0A_CM0707_C01.pdf
4. http://carlarieger.com/blog/why-is-fun-at-work-so-important/

Lightning Source UK Ltd.
Milton Keynes UK
UKHW011356201219
355748UK00002B/664/P